HERTFORDSHIRE LIBRARY

WITHDRAWN FOR SALE
PRICE: £1·00

SOLD

POST O

Getting the
MESSAGE

The Story of the British Post Office

Christopher Browne is a journalist who writes for The Times, The Sunday Times *and the* Daily Telegraph. *He is a former sub-editor on the* Daily Telegraph *Weekend section, caption writer on the* Evening Standard *and deputy features editor of the Liverpool* Daily Post. *He writes short stories for children and has published a book of humorous poetry.*

Getting the
MESSAGE

The Story of the British Post Office

Christopher Browne

HERTFORDSHIRE
LIBRARY SERVICE

No.

Class
383'. 4941

Supplier	Price	Date
JMLS	£14.99	03194

ALAN SUTTON

First published in the United Kingdom in 1993 by
Alan Sutton Publishing Limited
Phoenix Mill · Far Thrupp · Stroud · Gloucestershire

First published in the United States of America in 1993 by
Alan Sutton Publishing Inc. · 83 Washington Street · Dover · NH 03820

Copyright © Christopher Browne, 1993

All rights reserved. No part of this publication may be reproduced, stored in a
retrieval system, or transmitted, in any form or by any means, electronic,
mechanical, photocopying, recording or otherwise, without the prior
permission of the publishers and copyright holders.

British Library Cataloguing in Publication Data

Browne, Christopher
Getting the Message: Story of the British Post Office
I. Title
383.4941

ISBN 0–7509–0351–1

Library of Congress Cataloging in Publications Data

Browne, Christopher, 1946–
Getting the message: the story of the British Post Office
Christopher Browne.
p. cm.
Includes bibliographical references and index.
ISBN (invalid) 0–7501–0351–1
1. Great Britain. Post Office–History. 2. Postal service–Great Britain–History. I. Title.
HE6935.B76 1993
383'.4941–dc20 93–1638
CIP

Typeset in 10/14 pt Times.
Typesetting and origination by
Alan Sutton Publishing.
Printed in Great Britain by
The Bath Press, Avon.

To John Lucas

Contents

List of Illustrations

Acknowledgements

The author would like to give special thanks to Jean Young Farrugia and the staff of Post Office Archives for their care, insight and humour.

Unless otherwise stated, all illustrations have been reproduced by kind permission of the Post Office, who reserve copyright.

1
Messengers with Winged Feet

My days are quicker than a post; they flee away.

Job

We are all communicators. We communicate in many different ways, and in the past fifty years our methods have become more and more sophisticated – aided by robots, computers and automation. Be it simple, complex, predictable or unexpected, the way we make contact helps to direct our and the world's destiny. We have fax systems that can reprint documents thousands of miles away; we have telephones which make contact via highly developed satellites; we have computers that transmit messages over huge networks; and we have a Post Office that delivers sixty-one million items a day. This lightning technology is based on centuries of research, trial and error – and failure. There was the German who tried to create a rocket post that exploded on take-off; the seventeenth-century French letter-boxes that turned into nesting places for mice; and Victorian telephone companies who removed their rivals' cables during skirmishes on London rooftops.

Today's systems stem from such primitive forms of contact as rocks left outside caves to show whether the inhabitants are at home; symbols like feathers, pieces of bark and stones used by American Indians when tracking their quarries; smoke signals wafting from hill to hill; quivers of arrows warning of approaching enemy tribes; the echo of drumbeats reverberating from village to village; and the columns of fire that are said to have guided the early Israelites out of the Sinai desert.

But the world's first letter-writers were a group of wealthy Syrian merchants who, wishing to pass on idle gossip between towns, villages and seaports, sent messages on animal hides via a team of runners with onyx cylinders round their necks. This was around 3800 BC. Then a village of ingenious Chinamen began sending news via carrier pigeons. The birds could travel thousands of miles and held messages in tiny cylinders under their wings, with whistles and bells dangling from their tail-feathers to ward off hostile eagles and hawks.

The pigeon later became a major message carrier during the Second World War.

Greece was the first nation to take more than a passing interest in message-carrying. Their runners, who were called *hemerodromes*, the Greek word for messengers, were used to pass on news to and from the armies of the early Greek empire (1600–400 BC). Some of their feats were as remarkable as the legendary Greek fables. Perhaps the most tragic occurred when hemerodrome Euchidas was sent to the Oracle at Delphi to fetch holy fire to mark the Greeks' victory over the Persians at the Battle of Salamis in 479 BC. While handing over the sacred torch to King Xerxes at the end of his 125 mile trip, the runner promptly fell down dead at his feet with exhaustion.

The Greek rulers seem to have adopted a pretty ruthless approach to their runners, for many of them died or suffered strokes after their marathon missions. In fact one such journey led to the founding of the famous marathon race. After the Greek army had successfully repulsed a force of 6,000 Persians, a soldier named Pheidippides was sent to Athens from the little village of Marathon to warn the Athenian king of an impending invasion of Persian ships. The runner successfully completed his 26 mile journey, arriving at the king's palace with the words: 'Rejoice, we conquer', before he, too, fell lifeless to the ground.

To mark the event, the Greeks held annual 26 mile marathons, featuring the top athletes of the day. And the annual marathon became one of the highlights of the early Olympic Games held near Mount Olympus and was later included in the modern Olympics. However, the Olympic marathon became a little more stamina-sapping when an extra 385 yd were added at the 1908 London Olympics so that the great race could finish in front of King Edward VII's royal box at the White City stadium.

We find the first signs of a contemporary postal system in the Bible. The word post – from the Latin word *positus*, meaning place – was first used in the Old Testament, and on one occasion, the prophet Job was heard to say: 'My days are swifter than a post, they flee away', while Second Chronicles 30:6 records: 'So the posts went with the letters from King Hezekiah and his princes throughout all Israel and Judah, according to the commandments of the king.' Chronicles also discloses that the prophets Jeremiah and Samuel, and St Paul the Apostle in the New Testament, sent letters via riders on horses, mules and young dromedaries, with rest-houses set up to provide new animals about a day's journey apart, a transport system first introduced by the Persians in 600 BC.

Biblical messages were usually sent on clay tablets, and occasionally slate, lead, copper, bronze or even wax ones on which the news could be scratched, then smoothed over and used again. However, the early Egyptian dynasties graduated from tablets to rough parchment from the dried hides of sheep, goats and calves and a light material, papyrus – the forerunner of paper – which they made out of reeds growing on the banks of the River Nile. They also cut out reed pens and mixed inks from vegetable dyes for their letters which they wrote in hieroglyphics – or pictures and symbols – instead of words.

Many of the Egyptian rider-messengers carried more than one hundredweight of messages in relays along the Nile's banks, while foot messengers faced long treks over hills and through woods and valleys. Any carrier about to set out on a particularly hazardous route would make out a will leaving his most valued possessions to his next of kin, in case he was killed by wild animals or robbers.

It was the Romans who changed this early relay system into a multi-rider network, with changes of rider and animal at each stopover. It meant greater distances could be covered more quickly. The journeys, however, were no safer. Riders often had to venture through enemy territory, risking capture, having their thumbs cut off or being tortured to death.

The Romans also used their messenger services to devise royal plots, and many a conspiracy was either won, lost or foiled at the drop of a letter, after the plotters had hidden their messages in the soles of their slaves' sandals. But, as an occupation, letter-carrying was rather frowned on by the Romans. Only the wealthiest nobleman could afford his own letter-carrier, and any slave who forgot to wake his master in the morning or to announce the arrival of an important visitor was ordered to carry letters as a punishment.

Foot messengers were eventually abolished by Emperor Augustus (63 BC–14 AD). Instead, he introduced the world's first man-made postal carrier – the chariot. The early ones were rudimentary horse-drawn carts. However they were later modified into sleek-looking carriages that attracted large crowds as they cruised into the Roman cities and towns with news of battles, invasions, sporting achievements and the Emperor Augustus's state of health. Some of the longer, more newsworthy narratives were written by the poet-philosophers Cicero, Pliny and Seneca and have become historical masterpieces.

La poste sous Auguste.

Slow Coach. The first man-made mail carrier was the Roman chariot. Introduced by Emperor
Augustus around 52 BC, it was noisy, cumbersome and slow

Towards the end of the Roman Empire a trend was emerging. The post was
influencing the growth of civilization. It was bringing key announcements and
news of other nations to rulers and noblemen to help them expand their trading
links and resources. As each empire – and nation – developed, so did its
message-carrying system and vice versa; when it declined, its post did
likewise. It is a trend we have seen during the last two centuries in Britain.
After the industrial revolution, the communicative powers of post and
telephone helped boost British business. Then 100 years later, during the
instability of the stop–go 1970s, the post suffered, only to revive again during
the booming 1980s.

Thus it was not surprising that when the Roman Empire fell, its postal
service faded. No big issues needed reporting, no achievements required the
impact of announcement, and no great battles inspired the public imagination.
There was a pause in message-carrying for several hundred years.

It was left to the seventh-century Arabic Empire to continue spreading the word. A word that helped to further the Muslim cause and made the *Tales of the Arabian Nights*, a book that has lulled many a British child to sleep, so popular. It was a golden era of ideas, invention and experiment when civilization and its favourite medium, letter-writing, flourished.

The Muslims used papyrus and Chinese paper for writing their messages and a two-tier system for delivering them. On longer journeys, Chinese-style carrier pigeons, with cylinders under their wings, flew the news over hazardous mountain and valley regions, while, on more straightforward missions, relays of horse riders sped across the sandy plains.

Aptly enough, the Muslims set up their first posts in Syria, the source of the world's first letter-carriers, soon adding Egypt and Palestine to their new relay network. Under the supervision of the Arab rulers or caliphs (the rightly-ruled), the Arabic post filtered through to central Asia and India and then to France and Spain in Europe. By the eighth and ninth centuries the Muslim post had grown into a network of nine hundred relay stations. Then suddenly in the tenth century, the Arabic Empire declined almost as rapidly as it had grown, and its post with it. But it had managed to leave its mark on Europe where a few Muslim messengers were still in service.

At that time the idea of sending handwritten messages would have been a pretty remote one to the average European. Most were poor, illiterate peasants who lived off the land in sectors – or tithes – owned by landlords, and subsisted on ground crops, lived in primitive self-built dwellings and used handmade tools for work and crude weapons for protection.

It was the Roman Catholic Church that fostered the first regular postal services. Wishing to spread Catholicism across Europe, its senior members founded monastic orders like the Carthusians, Benedictines and Cistercians who started little communities called monasteries. Soon the monastery heads, or abbots, found they needed to contact their contemporaries with news items, such as the names of recently deceased monks or the opening of new monasteries. So they began sending messages written on parchment scrolls, using their lay monks as postmen. Each monastery would then add its own topics of interest and the scrolls became longer and longer. One that was sent to mark the death of St Vitus, carried a hundred news items and measured 28 ft when it reached its destination at a small French Benedictine monastery.

In denser population areas, arable land became sparse, and people began

Post Haste. A speeding post-boy wakes up a toll-keeper in the middle of the night with a blast on his bugle

trading in goods and services. Larger communities, or towns, began to grow and attracted people with a thirst for knowledge. But, as teachers had nowhere to teach and students nowhere to learn, the two groups decided to pool their resources and set up learning centres, or universities. The main ones were at Bologna, Paris and Oxford. Many of the professors and students were a long way from home, so they wrote letters which they sent via teams of university couriers, or letter-doctors as they were known. Though there were only two deliveries a year, the letter-doctors were held in high esteem, often making friends with the young men of letters and helping them with their studies. Perhaps the most famous was Oxford's John Barefoot, who was renowned for his remarkable memory.

Sometimes letter-doctors carried letters for local townsfolk. The idea caught on, and within a few years many a town was running its own messenger service. The new town couriers were often divided into different trades, such as bakers, shoemakers and blacksmiths. One team that served a group of butchers in the German Lowlands was called the Butchers' Post. Not only did its messengers have to be expert horsemen, they also had to spend several months in the German cavalry. Soon they became famous for carrying the world's first post-horns which they blew on entering a town. But perhaps the most effective courier service of the era was Germany's Hanseatic League which added military might to its postal pluck by sending a soldier with each messenger to protect him from robbery or attack by rival traders.

By the thirteenth and fourteenth centuries the European posts had begun to join up like the links of a chain. Two countries, Italy and Spain, formed their own national networks and gave their messengers the more superior-sounding title, couriers. They carried letters written on parchment and sealed with wax, in open sacks and charged the recipients high fees. But their work did not always stop at delivery. They often had to read out the letters to their addressees as few could yet read or write.

On longer missions couriers were armed with long spears to protect them from ambush and attack, though, when visiting important clients, they would often use the spear-tips to present the post as a mark of respect. On shorter missions couriers carried poles to help them cross rivers and fords, an idea that later developed into the modern pole-vault.

Letters that were not individually delivered were taken to a collection point in town where people could pick them up; while at local ports, sea-going merchants were paid to carry letters overseas for townsfolk and traders, the most famous being the Strangers' Post based at the Port of London.

The largest medieval network was the Taxis Post, which began in Innsbruck, Austria, and was named after an Italian family of couriers known as Tassi, or badgerskins, which they wore on their foreheads to deflect falling branches and flying insects. In 1505 Franz, the family head, was asked by the German government to start a national postal system. So he devised a highly efficient relay network in which both riders and horses were changed at posts – or change-over points – each courier carrying his letters in a robber-proof leather pouch, known as a mail, and recording his transactions in a log-book.

The only official users of the Taxis Post were the courtiers of the German

Useful Tip. Seventeenth-century couriers often used the tips of their spears to deliver letters to noblemen as a mark of respect

emperor, Maximilian I, though it also carried post for other monarchies, sometimes taking the letters of King Henry VIII to members of the French and Spanish royal families. The public were not allowed to use the service, though it is obvious that a few discreet deals were made on the side with Taxis postmen.

As it spread across Europe the Taxis Post created its own postal routes, over which it had virtual monopoly. If a Taxis courier met another on his travels, he would attack him and steal his post, and, in heavily wooded areas, the German couriers would sometimes ambush their unsuspecting rivals. The Taxis Post's aggression put some couriers out of business, while others competed by charging lower rates. However, it succeeded in forging Europe's first postal routes and by the mid-seventeenth century its twenty thousand blue- and silver-uniformed couriers were covering most of Europe.

During the sixteenth and seventeenth centuries several large networks began operating in Europe, the most distinctive of which was the Swiss Post whose couriers carried the coats-of-arms and colours of their native towns. Though most letters were about practical matters of state, some were downright personal, such as one in which King Louis XIII of France told a senior bishop that if he did not mend his ways, he would be thrown into the River Seine and left to drown. The bishop replied: 'I can assure the King that if he does do what he promiseth, I shall arrive more quickly in Paradise by my watery route than he by his postal horses.' Perhaps the most unique city network began in Paris. Called *La Petite Post*, it boasted the world's first post-boxes as well as a team of couriers who collected and delivered the post three times a day. The man credited with the idea was an inventor called Monsieur Renouard de Velayer, who is also reputed to have made the first clock with luminous dials and to have created the first lift, which shortly after being installed at Versailles palace infuriated King Louis XIV when his favourite mistress was stuck for three hours between floors.

'The Little Post' was launched in 1653. The same day, de Velayer sent a circular to his fellow Parisians saying that the new service was for

> those who have no valets, those who have valets that are ill or needed in the house; those whose servants are lazy or like to take a stroll and afterwards say they could not find the address; the merchant who does not wish to leave his shop for fear of losing clients; those who are in someone else's service, like all domestic servants who have not the

liberty to leave the house; those who are troubled by bad health or by their creditors; those who are shut up in prisons, in religious houses or colleges which have no valets.

La Petite Post was given an enthusiastic reception. But a few days later a group of practical jokers put mice in its eleven iron post-boxes, so that when the couriers arrived they found a few bits of unreadable parchment and several nests at the bottom. The 'joke' was repeated night after night, and soon *La Petite Post* became *La Très Petite Post*. The inventive de Velayer desperately searched for solutions. Failing to find any, he closed the service three months later, and *La Petite Post* became *La Post Morte*.

Meanwhile, across the Atlantic, another network had sprung up. The North American Post was started by the first British settlers and leased to an American tenant by the British government for 6*s* a year. However, the omens did not look too good when the first one, Thomas O'Neale, made a loss in each of his first two years, and died in a state of dire poverty. His successors fared better, starting a dual-purpose messenger and rider system that continued until the American War of Independence, after which the American government took control.

At first the post's American owners found they were spending most of their time trying to keep out corrupt elements and illegal letter-opening by power-hungry political groups. It led one despairing postal official to remark, 'There is too much curiosity about the sentiments of public men.' However, the senders got wise to the corruption and began writing letters in special codes.

As the American frontiers opened up, so did the post, and soon rider services were operating half-way across North America. The most famous was the Pony Express, launched in 1860 to link Missouri in central North America to California on the west coast, a 1,966 mile route across American Indian territory. The Express's exploits have become the stuff of romance, one gallant rider being ambushed and shot six times in a canyon by cattle rustlers before successfully reaching the next relay-point with all his post intact. The serpent-like Pony Express was served by 100 riders, 400 horses and 190 relay-stations.

The other main North American network was the Wells Fargo, whose stage-coaches also became symbols of Wild West daring and adventure. A private service, it had offices all over North America that doubled as passenger depots and post offices, and it worked in tandem with the government post, charging

Presidential Post. Abraham Lincoln used to deliver letters to the local folk when he was working as a postmaster in New Salem, Illinois

normal letter rates plus a very large fee for the privilege of travelling 'Wells Fargo'. Eventually the network was absorbed by the state post.

North America's most distinguished postmaster was Abraham Lincoln. 'Honest Abe' – as he was known – owned a shop in New Salem, Illinois, and in 1833, when he was twenty-three, Lincoln was asked to be the town's postmaster. His tall, gangling figure became a feature of the town, as he handed out postal items from a large battered hat, often stopping to chat with the townsfolk or helping the blacksmith with his shoeing. Sometimes when visiting the more remote farms and cabins, where the folk were illiterate, Lincoln would read out their letters to them, embellishing the scripts with a few stories of his own, then helping the grateful villagers to compose their replies.

When he became a postmaster, Lincoln was able to shrug off his humble log-cabin origins and educate himself by reading the local newspapers and learning how to write articles and make speeches. In fact, Lincoln's spell as a postmaster marked the start of his political career and, after joining the Republican Party in 1856, the former postmaster was elected president in 1860. In his presidential address, he paid tribute to the postal system he had helped develop.

2
Kingdom of the Couriers

To meete with the dangerous and secret intelligence of ill-affected persons, both at home and abroad, by the over great liberty taken both in writing and riding in poste, especially in and through our countie of Kent.

Proclamation by King Charles I, 1632

A few royal horsemen carrying letters for the king was the nearest Britain came to a postal system in the medieval ages. She was an island with few influences and rare intruders, lacking the rivalries and religious movements of the volatile European posts. Ironically it was war that inspired Britain's first real attempt at an organized post. In 1482 King Edward IV sent teams of couriers to Scotland to spread propaganda during the Anglo-Scottish civil war in the misguided belief that they would form themselves into a proper network. But most of the couriers were either captured or killed and it proved a fruitless exercise.

So the medieval British courier carried on treading a lonely, unsung trail,

Personal Service. A fifteenth-century messenger politely doffs his cap as he delivers a letter to the royal court

First Post. King Henry VIII was the first English monarch to take letter-carrying seriously when he allowed noblemen and merchants to use the royal post (by courtesy of the National Portrait Gallery, London)

Master's Touch. The role of the first master of the posts, Sir Brian Tuke, was fairly limited as he had only twenty letter-carriers working for him though one named Croylande wrote proudly in his diary that he and his colleagues carried considerable political weight and travelled at the 'utmost speede'. It is safe to assume, however, that they rode in 20 mile relays at speeds of about 15 miles per hour.

The father of the British postal system is King Henry VIII. In 1512, three years after coming to the throne, he recruited a team of twenty horsemen to work as his official royal couriers and appointed Sir Brian Tuke, his chief treasurer and clerk of the signet, Master of the Posts. Tuke replaced the relay-points with post-houses – inns and taverns at 30 mile intervals – where couriers could change over in comfort. The innkeepers became the first postmasters, their role being to collect the post, give the couriers refreshments and supply fresh horses. On shorter journeys, ten- to eleven-year-old boys carried the post on foot. They also guided the mounted couriers along poorly marked tracks, sometimes bringing their tired horses back to the inns.

Battles were good news sources, and during Anglo-Scottish and French conflicts like the Battle of Spurs and the Battle of Flodden, Henry VIII would set up special battlefield postal services to give him progress reports on the fighting and make urgent requests for reinforcements. Ever since early Greece's Battle of Marathon, war and all its influences has played an important role in the post's development.

However, carrying the post in the sixteenth century could be a thankless task. When he arrived at the post-house, the courier was invariably dirty and dishevelled from his ride on the rough roads, his horse was often lame, and he was sometimes the victim of mischief-makers. When he had got his breath back, the newly arrived courier had to produce a passport that he was of 'one able horse payeing at the rate of one penny by the myle, being sent about the Kinges Majesties affairs'. He then handed the contents of his mail-bag to the postmaster who wrote on the face of each letter the date and time of its receipt and recorded the distance it had travelled in a log-book, keeping his local letters and handing items bound for other areas to the outgoing courier.

At that time the posts were irregular, and though Tuke painted a rather rosier picture to the king, 'Many time happen two depeches [despatches] in a day one way and sometimes more', couriers often failed to visit an area for several months, which meant the postmasters lost their retainers for supplying horses. Such delays could also prove disheartening for senders of urgent letters who would write: 'Haste, post haste', on the front, or in very urgent cases: 'Haste, haste, haste, for lyfe, for lyfe, haste!'

However, the service had a limited clientele. The only people allowed to send letters – single, folded sheets of rag-paper with red wax seals – were the king and his court and noblemen and merchants, who had to get the king's special permission. Though, unknown to Tuke and the king, a number of private couriers were taking messages for members of the public. When Henry VIII found out about them, he opened the royal post to the public. People could now visit their local post-houses to pick up their letters, paying the postmaster for each one, and depositing any they wished to send.

After the accession of Queen Elizabeth I, merchants and businessmen began sending letters overseas, despatching them via courier to Dover where they would be carried by Dutch or Spanish merchant vessels. However, believing the letters carried subversive or anti-government propaganda, the queen passed an Act in 1591 stating that all overseas post must be carried by British vessels only.

Another element of Elizabethan corruption was letter-spying – by both government and public alike. Though Queen Elizabeth I herself used it during her famous quarrel with Mary, Queen of Scots. While Mary and her forty-strong household were held under house arrest in several English estates and castles, Elizabeth I ordered that all letters sent to Mary by foreign Catholics should be opened by a specially-appointed officer. Elizabeth then used them as

Royal Reformer. Queen Elizabeth I removed many of the royal post's corrupt elements and increased the number of mounted couriers to a hundred

Fatal Seal. Letters sent by foreign Catholics to Mary, Queen of Scots, led to her execution when they were opened by one of Queen Elizabeth I's court officers

evidence at the Scottish queen's trial, which led to her execution for treason.

By the end of her reign Queen Elizabeth had managed an effective clean-up of the post and also boosted its workforce to one hundred. When her successor, James I, came to the throne and found a flurry of private couriers threatening the royal post's revenues, he passed an Act banning them altogether, including the Strangers' Post of merchants and bankers at the Port of London (see Chapter 1). The royal post was now a monopoly.

The People's Post

Postal values have changed in the past four hundred years. In the seventeenth century a recipient was quite satisfied if his letter arrived five days after it was posted. Today the customer expects all his letters to arrive the next day. Imagine what would have happened if news of the French king, William the Conqueror's arrival in 1066 had reached King Harold and his troops in York, in twenty-four hours, instead of the five days it actually took. We might never have had a Norman invasion and British history could have taken a very different course.

In the seventeenth century getting a letter was a rare treat and often a source of great excitement, but the means of taking it from A to B needed a lot of

Public Post. King Charles I started a
national letter-writing trend when he
created the Post Office in 1635

plain hard work. Like his father, James I, King Charles I was a zealous postal reformer. In 1632 he appointed two masters of the post, Thomas Witherings, a former London mercer, and William Frizell, to 'carry out the King's wishes' and 'to meete with the dangerous and secret intelligence of ill-affected persons, both at home and abroad, by the over great liberty taken both in writing and riding in poste, especially in and through our countie of Kent', which, put simply, meant they had to curb private letter-carrying.

In 1635 King Charles passed an Act of Parliament officially opening the royal post to all members of the British public. He called the network the Post Office. All carriers were to be referred to as post-boys and all postmasters were ordered to have 'sufficient horses and messengers alwaies in readinesse to go forth with the pacquets without aine delay and to deliver them from stage to stage within the compasse of an hour and a half for everie stage'. A large post-house was opened in Bishopsgate, London, to distribute overseas items 'for way of Antwerp everie Friday, for way of France everie Wednesday and for that of Holland everie Saturday'.

The public were now spared the high fees of the private courier. In the new Post Office, each item had a set rate. A single sheet travelling up to 80 miles cost 2d; from 80 to 140 miles, 4d; and 140 miles plus, 6d; letters to Scotland were 8d, and Ireland, 9d. All postage was paid by the recipient. Rates were based on a simple economic equation, mileage, for Witherings estimated that carrying letters by post-horse cost 2½d per mile – a tiny expense when divided by the number of items they carried.

Under Witherings's stewardship the Post Office began to spread its tentacles. As well as the main postal routes, Witherings set up smaller 'by-posts' on side roads and more out-of-the-way routes where, as well as his mail-bag, each post-boy wore a by-bag full of local letters round his waist.

The public was delighted with the new service and, in 1640, King Charles sent a circular to all postmasters (and several new postmistresses) that 'any man may with safetie and securitie send letters to any part of this Kingdom and receive an answer within five days'. This was often the case, though during the winter mounted post-boys were sometimes delayed by heavy snowfalls and severe frosts and, sometimes tarried with their friends on the by-roads, got drunk in the local taverns or had to walk when their horses became lame.

When civil war reared its ugly head in 1642, Oliver Cromwell and his parliamentary forces, the Roundheads, tried to take control of the post. Posses of Roundheads would gallop along the highways, stopping post-boys, taking their mail-bags and transferring them to their own couriers. After his defeat of Charles I's Cavaliers in 1649, Cromwell passed an Act giving Parliament power to open letters 'to discover and prevent many dangerous and wicked designes which have been and are daily contrived against the peace and welfare of this commonwealth'.

He also appointed Isaac Dorislaus as the government's official letter-opener. Dorislaus had a secret room next to the Foreign Office, and each night at 11 p.m., after the last post had been collected, he would check each item of outgoing government mail, opening any suspicious-looking items or those he believed might pose a threat to the state. In his first six months, Dorislaus opened 185 government letters, passing on their contents to Cromwell, now head of state.

In some ways Cromwell proved to be as effective a postal reformer as Charles I. In 1653 he made the Post Office a franchise, appointing John Manley its first tenant for an annual rental of £10,000 and giving him strict orders to arrest anyone carrying the post illegally. One day, Manley and Edmond Prideaux, master of the inland posts, were tipped off about a pirate group based at a house in London and

did, in ryotous manner, with swords and other weapons, by force breake into the house where the goods and letters of the Undertakers (private couriers) were and thrust their servants out of doors and after threatening speeches and many more outrages committed, required the Undertakers to receive no more letters.

Cromwell liked to court the approval of the rich, famous and successful. He thus decided to introduce franking, or free postage, for Members of Parliament (MPs), noblemen, and their wealthy friends. They merely had to endorse the backs of their letters with their signatures to qualify for free postage. He also passed a law donating £5,382 10s of the Post Office's annual profits to the current ruler or head of state. Later, the annual donation was raised, until the government was able to take a large percentage of the Post Office's profits – reducing the amount it could spend on its own upkeep.

In 1657 Cromwell and his government passed the Post Office Act. London's main post-house in Bishopsgate became the General Post Office (GPO), responsible for sorting all letters to the provincial towns, and John Thurloe, Cromwell's secretary of state, was appointed Postmaster-General. Sadly, Thurloe's career was short-lived. Cromwell died in 1658, to be succeeded by his son Richard, who was, in turn, overthrown by King Charles II in 1660. Charles's first act was to pass a Post Office Charter, dismissing Thurloe and appointing Colonel Henry Bishop, of Henfield, Sussex, as his new postmaster-general. Bishop also took over Manley's tenancy of the Post Office for £21,500 a year.

However, Bishop had a tricky task in front of him. A new scourge had emerged at the Post Office – internal crime. A number of post-boys had reported seeing postmasters stealing the contents of money-letters. One of the

Rent-a-Post. Oliver Cromwell made the Post Office a franchise operation in 1653 when he leased it out to John Manley for £10,000 a year (reproduced by courtesy of the Bodleian Library; 8vo 0 156 BS(2) (frontispiece))

Top Marks. Colonel Henry Bishop, the Post Office's second franchisee, introduced the first postmark – a circle in the top right-hand corner of a letter showing the date and place of posting

worst offenders was said to be Loughborough's postmaster, John Cobley, who was 'taking corn of some, hay of others and money of all, for all the couriers must stop at his house.' There were also complaints about the service. On one occasion, Colonel Roger Whitley, the deputy postmaster-general, had to write to Lechlade's postmistress: 'I am creditably informed that your horse tired at Lechlade this week, and that the courier was supplied with one out of a cart. This is scandalous!' And he told another:

> I am informed that you never have a horse in your stable and that the ostler (the inn's stableman) has sometimes had to travel three miles to fetch one from grass. This is very unsatisfactory and must be put right immediately.

Canterbury's postmaster, meanwhile, was given a severe reprimand by Colonel Whitley for sending mail by 'a strange Dutchman without a guide'. The colonel's remedy was to visit all the post-houses, speaking to, and if necessary, arresting the postmasters and mistresses.

Some postmasters had more harmless reputations. Mr Tobias Hobson, of Cambridge, a jolly and friendly man who liked a joke, supervised all changes of horse at the stable adjoining his inn. Whenever a post-boy came to pick up a steed,

Hobson would give him the one nearest the stable-door. If the post-boy did not like the animal he was given, he had to go without – a practice that became known as 'Hobson's Choice'. Another postmaster, James Brewster, of Scrooby, Nottinghamshire, who was a Quaker, was offered a pay rise after he put up King James II on the way to his accession, but turned it down on 'religious grounds'. Brewster was one of the Pilgrim Fathers, and later became head of a settlement in New Plymouth, USA.

In his second year of office, Bishop introduced the postmark. A stamp

> is invented that is putt upon every letter showing the day of the moneth that every letter comes to the office, so that no Letter Carrier may dare detayne a letter from post to post, which before was usual.

It consisted of a small circle showing the date and place of posting stamped in the right-hand corner of each letter. As Post Office volumes rose, some post-houses found they were facing almost impossible workloads, so Bishop opened a series of letter-receiving houses – usually a small room in a private house – to help handle the rising traffic.

Soon Bishop's Post Office was not only covering its overheads and paying a retainer to the king, it was also showing a small profit. However, its satisfaction was soured by yet more postal pirates. Despite two laws abolishing them, private couriers were still plying their trade, even setting up their own little networks with post-houses and postmasters. So Charles II passed the third Parliament Act to ban 'the secret conveyance of the mails'. Suspects were arrested, tried before a special Post Office council and, if found guilty, sent to prison.

This time the medicine worked, and the Post Office could hold its head high again. However, fate intervened again when two natural – rather than man-made – hazards upset its smooth rate of progress. In 1665 the Bubonic Plague, introduced by rats from the continent, raged through London, killing thousands of residents and maiming many others. To prevent it spreading, a three week curfew was imposed on all outgoing letters, while internal mail items had to be individually 'aired over vinegar' and delivered at the ends of poles in case of contamination. Though the Plague's effects were short-lived, it took several months for the London post to return to normal. And scarcely had it done so than in 1666 the Great Fire of London raged through the capital, engulfing the Bishopsgate GPO in its flaming wake. All the GPO's employees managed to flee to safety, but tens of thousands of letters were destroyed, and the office had to be temporarily moved to Bridges Street, re-opening twelve years later in Lombard Street.

3
Heroes and Highwaymen

We muffled up with cape and handkerchief and overtook them, but the
gentlemen put their bodies out of the coach and fired both at once.
Diary of an anonymous highwayman, 1667

With more than a hundred routes at its disposal and a growing network of
post- and letter-receiving houses, the seventeenth-century Post Office rivalled
the European posts in size and capacity. More and more people were learning
to read and write, jotting down their news and views instead of making long
journeys to visit relatives and friends. Several large towns had two or three
deliveries a week and most villages were getting a service. There were still
large gaps, however. For instance, it was very difficult for people living in the
same town to make contact. In London, which had half-a-million inhabitants
– one-tenth of Britain's population – letters often provided crucial links
between traders, the professions and large business institutions. But, though
Londoners could make contact with other towns, they could not contact one
another.

Dirty Work. A highwayman bent
on robbery

However, history has a habit of finding solutions. This time it was a case of 'cometh the time, cometh the man'. In 1680 London merchant William Dockwra approached the government with a plan to divide London into ten postal districts. It met with their approval and Dockwra put his plan into action, converting four hundred private houses, taverns, inns and offices into 'receiving-houses' and introducing a penny post for all London mail under an ounce. Letters were to be prepaid, the sender handing his penny to the postmaster at his local receiving-house. Instead of a circle, letters were stamped with a triangle, which also showed the first letter of the district in which they were posted (i.e. W for Wandsworth). Couriers, who travelled on foot, visited the receiving-houses hourly, picking up the post and taking it to Lombard Street's district office ready for distribution. London traders and businessmen now had a first-class city network. Each day there were between eight and twelve deliveries, and many items were sent and delivered the same day. By the end of 1680 a million letters had been delivered by district postmen. Even the London porters, who had previously sneered on the city postmen as a bunch of opportunists, decided to join the new network.

The London writer Daniel Defoe was moved to write:

Postal Pundit. The writer Daniel Defoe was so impressed by London's penny post that he described it as a 'testimony of the greatness of this city'

The Penny Post . . . though for a time it was subject to miscarriages and mistakes, yet now it is come also into so exquisite a management that nothing can be more exact and 'tis with the utmost safety and dispatch that letters are delivered to the remotest corners of town, almost as soon as they can be sent by a messenger, and that four, five, six to eight times a day, according as the distance of the place makes it practicable . . . I mention this the more particularly because it is so manifest a testimony of the greatness of this city, and to the great extent of the Business and Commerce of it, that this Penny Conveyance should raise so many thousand pounds a year, and employ so many poor people in the diligence of it as this office employs. We see nothing of this at Paris, Amsterdam, or any other city.

Many London residents, however, were unsure of the time of the last posts, and it was left to a London businessman, Charles Povey, to ring the changes. He put bell-ringers at several street corners in Southwark and Westminster, who, just before the last post at 8 p.m., would start jangling their bells to arouse last-minute letter-writers. Soon the chimes of the bellmen as they collected the late post resonated all over London – and later Edinburgh, Manchester, Bristol and Birmingham, when they too adopted penny posts.

Another London reform was the opening of a Money Order Office. Post-boys were carrying an increasing number of letters holding money and valuables like gold rings and watches, often with dire consequences. Senders were now able to buy special money orders, which they would sometimes send in two separate halves to prevent theft. The Post Office also introduced registered money letters for members of the overseas forces who wished to send wages home.

Meanwhile Bishop had stumbled on an idea to extend the Post Office's rural delivery fleet. He introduced what can only be described as crude-looking four-wheeled carts with wide canopies, which were drawn by a pair of overweight drays. The carts, which were used for long-distance travel by the working classes, were notoriously slow as the drays were rarely changed – and the impoverished passengers only agreed to take letters if they were paid handsomely for their pains. As there were no street numbers or names, senders had to give their carriers a very clear description of their letters' destinies such as 'The shop with the bright-yellow door near the clump of beech trees at the southern end of the main street in Breckington'. A letter might take several weeks in the hands of inexperienced messengers. In London, the elegant

Late Call. Businessman Charles Povey appointed bellmen to stand at London street corners to remind people to bring their letters in time for the last post

hackney carriages favoured by the upper classes, which had glass windows and were drawn by four horses, were also used for carrying items of mail. However, neither stage-wagons nor hackney carriages appealed to the postmasters as they detracted from their own postal and livery businesses.

Robbers of the Highway

As the wagons rattled and clattered over the stony roads, sometimes getting stuck in a rut or losing a wheel, they faced another obstacle – highwaymen. These sinister-looking figures would swoop like phantoms on unsuspecting wagons, threatening the drivers and passengers with blunderbusses and pistols. Then, after stealing money, jewellery and valuable postal packets, they would disappear into the night. The highwaymen often worked in respectable jobs during the day, meeting in the taverns at night, where they would don black cloaks, masks and tricorn hats before planning their cunning deeds. Their policy was to work in threes or fours, so that in rare cases of resistance they could defend themselves.

Occasionally the robbers of the highway held up post-boys, one rider on the London to Gloucester road being held up and robbed eight times in two months.

The first known postal hold-up occurred in 1650 when highwaymen stole a letter containing elevenpence from a stage-wagon on London's Hampstead Heath. It was to be the first of many. One of the most notorious highwaymen remained anonymous until his death. However, he kept a diary of hold-ups over a twenty-year period, one of which occurred in 1667 when he and his accomplice, John Hawkins, stopped the hackney carriage of the Earl of Burlington and Lord Bruce in the woods of Richmond, Surrey.

> Me and my friend met a chariot with two bright gentlemen in it; as soon as ever they past us, we muffled up with cape and handkerchief and overtook them. I was on one side and Hawkins was on the other. Then they handed over the goods which were 20 pounds of money, two gold watches, a sapphire ring and some postal packets. But the gentlemen put their bodies out of the coach and fired both at once; one of them lodged three slugs in Hawkins's shoulder. We galloped off to prevent murder on both sides.

Toll Fee. A caricature by the artist Thomas Rowlandson of a young lady paying the bellman his penny fee for collecting her letter

Daylight Robbery. A highwayman orders a startled
mail-coach passenger to hand over the money-letters

Hawkins was later hanged, while his anonymous accomplice lived to the
ripe old age of eighty-seven.

The most famous highwayman, Dick Turpin, carried out many successful
hold-ups with his two partners, Matthew King and Stephen Potter. One night,
as Turpin lay in wait for an unsuspecting stage-wagon in Epping Forest, the
forest keeper, Henry Thompson, became suspicious and crept up on him with a
gun. Turpin turned and promptly shot him dead. The next day a price of £200
was put on the highwayman's head. So he fled to Yorkshire, changed his name
to John Palmer and started trading as a horse dealer. One evening, Turpin was
seen shooting at a game-cock by farm labourer John Robinson who shouted at
him to stop. Turpin angrily pointed his gun at the labourer and threatened to
kill him. Recognizing the former highwayman, Robinson reported the incident
to the police, and Turpin was arrested and sent to York Castle prison.

While serving his sentence, Turpin received a summons to appear in court
on horse-stealing charges. In desperation, he wrote to his brother-in-law,
Pompadour Rivernall, an Essex lawyer, asking for his help. On receiving the
letter, Rivernall, who did not want to pay the postal charge, sent it back
unopened, assuming it meant all was well with Turpin. However, when the

Death Penalty. Britain's most notorious highwayman, Dick Turpin, sealed his fate with a letter about his crimes to his brother-in-law

letter arrived back at the local post-house, the postmaster, who happened to be Turpin's former schoolmaster James Smith, recognized the writing. Smith opened the letter and, after reading details of Turpin's crimes, reported him to the Yorkshire police. The highwayman was tried, found guilty and sentenced to hang. He was then taken to the gallows at York Tyburn, and after a few words with the hangman, when he is said to have confessed to his criminal past, threw himself off the scaffold ladder and died within three minutes.

By the end of the seventeenth century stage-wagons were carrying out an interrupted postal service on most of the major roads. Even though many passengers were armed, they found it difficult to compete with the lightning cunning of the highwaymen who would sometimes conduct little outdoor ceremonies, flirting, swooning and dancing with the female passengers before riding off with their ill-gotten gains. The government, therefore, decided to reinforce the wagons, toughening the sides with metal plates strong enough to resist blunderbuss bullets, and calling them 'robber-proof' carts.

Ralph 'The Reformer' Allen

Britain's landscape began to change, with its widening communications
network. More roads were built and industrial sites and factories opened
outside the larger towns, replacing cottage industries in some of the smaller
ones. A new commercial middle class emerged; people wanted to better
themselves and give their children a secure, dependable future in such
professions as the Law, the Church, medicine, and the forces, and in such
institutions as the Post Office. One particular individual, a successful Cornish
innkeeper named John Allen, was keen to forge a future for his son and, when
the lad was eleven, sent him to help his grandmother, who worked as a
postmistress at the little village of St Columb.

A conscientious worker, Ralph Allen was soon able to carry out many of his
grandmother's tasks, and at the age of nineteen became a postmaster in Bath,
where he earned a reputation as a fair and kindly boss and made a sizeable profit.
In 1719 the Post Office advertised for someone to take charge of the rural
network. Allen applied and got the job, agreeing as part of his contract to pay the
Post Office an annual rental of £6,000 a year; the rest was his own income.

Determined to keep the Post Office in profit and curb any crooked elements,
the young Allen appointed three travelling surveyors to search post-boys and
their mail-bags and ensure money-letters were not being tampered with.
Anyone found stealing a money-letter was hanged. Meanwhile, suspicion
continued to hover over the postmasters, whose reputation had hardly
improved in a hundred years, and Allen frequently heard reports of money-
letters going missing between post-houses. So he asked his surveyors to keep a
surveillance check on all postmasters and their receipts. On one occasion he
told the northern surveyor:

> As you pass through Doncaster, enquire why the postmistress there
> never accounts for any 'by-letters' received from Beverley for her own
> delivery, though it appears that several letters are constantly sent from
> thence to Beverley.

Ralph 'the reformer' Allen also appointed business managers to improve the
quality of service at major post- and receiving-houses. Soon standards began to

Reformer Extraordinaire. During his forty-one years as the Post Office's franchisee, Ralph Allen smartened up the post-houses, speeded up local deliveries, and streamlined the sea-going post with packet-boats

rise. This was perhaps not entirely unexpected as the managers were on incentive schemes, receiving 10 per cent of their annual profits as income. Allen's final security measure was the introduction of tough, purpose-built packet boats for overseas mail (see Chapter 9) after a spate of 'top security' government letters went missing.

Allen then set to work on the transport system, introducing daily deliveries from London to Bristol, Coventry and the new manufacturing town of Birmingham, and forging new postal routes to Wales, the West Country and the southern ports of Falmouth, Dover and Harwich. He also appointed an Edinburgh-based controller for Scotland, which had hitherto sent all its letters by private carrier, and created several Scottish postal routes. A total of four hundred postal routes now bisected Britain.

Ralph 'the reformer' Allen had laid several of the modern Post Office's foundations. When he retired in 1761, the post was making an annual profit of £31,000, from which he drew an income of £12,000, a considerable sum in those days. Allen, who had also served as the mayor of Bath, retired to his country-house near the city where he held lavish dinner parties for such friends

Theatrical Role. Henry Fielding based the character of Squire Allworthy in his play *Tom Jones* on Ralph Allen

as Sir William Pitt and the writers Jonathan Swift, Alexander Pope and Henry Fielding. In fact, Squire Allworthy in Fielding's play *Tom Jones*, is meant to have been based on Allen, 'a commoner raised higher above the multitude by superior talents than is the power of the price to exalt him; whose behaviour to those that he obliged is more amiable than the obligation itself.' While Pope paid tribute to his friend with an epigram:

> Let humble Allen, with an awkward shame,
> Do good by stealth, and blush to find it fame.

The First Newspapermen

Britain had grown into a nation of prospering agricultural hamlets and expanding towns. Fifteen per cent of the population were yeoman farmers; the squalor of the medieval villages had gone; Queen Anne style houses went up in London and the cities; many Scottish and Northern shires became country estates; a new squirearchy bought antiques in Europe and had a house in London and a place in the country. There was a moral and spiritual revival; churches had full congregations; groups of serious young men worked for the 'benefit of the community'; hospitals were built and children's homes opened to cope with the growing number of abandoned offspring; road tolls helped to improve the rough and pitted roads; schools were founded with ambitious curricula, and a good education became the apotheosis of British breeding. The foundations of the industrial revolution had been laid.

As communications improved, so did the public's thirst for idle gossip. Many a postmaster would jot down snatches of news or gossip he had overheard in his inn and give it to the post-boy who would then pass it on to the next village where an equally loquacious postmaster would do likewise, adding a few tit-bits of his own. And so it went on from village to village, town to town, and city to city, the tales becoming longer and livelier, and the notes spreadeagling on to several sheets of paper. By about the sixth town they had become action-packed newsletters. And so news travelled, the postmasters often adding their own titles like 'The Protestant Post-boy', 'The Postman' and 'The Flying Post'. Soon the idea aroused the commercial instincts of local businessmen who began printing newspapers on Caxton presses in the bigger towns and cities. Among the first was *The Times*, started in London on 1 January 1785. This early postal

Sheer Poetry. Alexander Pope wrote an epigram on Ralph Allen that went the rounds of the London coffee-houses

enterprise explains why so many of today's newspapers carry words like 'mail', 'post', 'messenger' and 'courier' in their titles.

The newspapers employed their own reporters and editors, and soon began recruiting foreign correspondents. To be seen reading a newspaper was at first regarded as rather highbrow, though more gossipy papers were later introduced to attract a wider audience. In 1785 the Post Office opened a Central Newspaper Office in London, with a staff of eighteen to handle the new fad. By the end of the year, three million newspapers had been despatched from London. Today, many newspapers and magazines are sent by post, though to qualify they must carry less than 67 per cent of advertising.

4

The Industrial Revelation

The Post Office seems to be bound to keep pace with the wonderful improvements with which the present age abounds.

Sir Francis Freeling, 1830

The Post Office was one of the pioneers of the Industrial Revolution. It forged new trading links, created a national news network and helped form many a happy personal relationship. But, like most great ideas, the Post Office had a flaw. It had a poor transport system. Its clumsy stage-wagons were described by the *Gentleman's Magazine* of 1771 as contraptions with 'wheels eight feet high and a body the same as a coal cart', while the mounted post-boys were often attacked by robbers and wayward travellers as they trotted along in their tin hats and huge boots stuffed with feet-warming hay.

New methods of transport were needed, and the answer came from an unlikely source – a bored young theatre manager in Bath who had been studying the postal system in his spare time. John Palmer drew up his own Plan for Reform, which he described as a radical alternative to the stage-wagon and 'the idle boy without character, mounted on a worn-out hack, who, so far from being able to defend himself or escape from a robber, is more likely to be in league with him'.

During a recent visit to France, Palmer had been impressed by the fast lightweight coaches used for mail-carrying. On his return, he conducted an experiment, travelling on all the main postal roads by stage-wagon, noting down the distances between towns and cities and the times of each journey. Then he approached the Chancellor of the Exchequer, Sir William Pitt, and pointed out the need to streamline postal deliveries with sleek French-style coaches. Pitt, for mainly political reasons, immediately took to the idea. His Whig government was under financial pressure, and he had been about to introduce a coal tax, which would have proved a very unpopular measure as coal was the main fuel source for homes and factories. Palmer's scheme gave him the perfect excuse to revive the government's revenue by raising postal charges instead of imposing a coal tax.

The Post Office management, however, was not in favour of the speedier

French coach. They believed a streamlined network would give good service to the larger towns and cities, but neglect the smaller ones, especially on rural by-roads served by by-posts. Nonetheless Pitt, who had recently become prime minister and wanted to remain popular, put the idea to the test. On the evening of 2 August 1784, a coach-and-four, with four passengers on board and ten mail-bags in its hold, set off from the Swan Tavern in Bristol. It travelled along the main post road to London, passing through Bath's famous Three Tuns Inn and continuing its long journey through the night down the Bath to London high road. Sixteen hours later, the coach arrived precisely on schedule at the Swan with Two Necks public house in Lechlade Lane, London, cheered over the last few miles by a large crowd of onlookers. The trial was a resounding success.

Pitt made Palmer Comptroller of the Mails, the London to Bristol service became a weekly one and new services were started from London to seventeen provincial towns and cities. The mail-coaches, which always carried a timepiece to make sure they were running on schedule, were hired from private

Quick Service. The first coach-and-four travelled from Bath to London in sixteen hours and managed to pick up several mail-bags on the way without stopping

contractors and travelled at speeds of 9 to 10 miles an hour, which a member of Pitt's government said was 'highly dangerous to the head, leading to an affectation of the brain'. The fastest coach, which operated between London and Devonport, was known as Quicksilver.

The new mail-coaches needed to be robber-proof; and Palmer again had the answer. He appointed scarlet-uniformed guards to sit over the mail at the rear, each of whom was armed with a blunderbuss, a pistol, two cutlasses, and a bugle to warn of attack or arrival in a new town. Some mischievous guards would shoot at passing chickens or give a toot on their bugles when they saw a pretty girl walking by. Several guards fell off, the only hint of their absence being a long and much cherished period of silence. The black-panelled coaches with their Royal Mail insignia and scarlet-clad guards had an aura of romance about them and local folk would gather excitedly whenever they arrived in town. The writer William Hazlitt said: 'Even the brother-in-law of a coachman in the Royal Post would regard himself as a person of importance.'

Over the next ten years Palmer's coaches replaced the robber-proof carts,

Last Resort. Highwaymen who tried to hold up mail-coaches suddenly discovered a new force to be reckoned with – armed guards. The guards, who sat over the post at the rear, often scared the highwaymen away

speeding up the national network and, despite the Post Office's earlier forebodings, providing a regular service on all the smaller by-roads. However, they were not weather-proof and sometimes fell foul of snowstorms. During a fierce blizzard in Edinburgh, the driver and guard were forced to abandon their coach and continue the journey on foot with the mail-bags over their shoulders. A few days later their frozen bodies were dug out of a snowdrift, though they had managed to lash the mail-bags to a roadside post. Perhaps the most dramatic postal delay occurred on Salisbury Plain. The Exeter mail-coach was nearing the end of its journey from London when a passenger looked out to see a lioness that had escaped from a local circus attacking one of the horses. He and his fellow passengers immediately jumped from the coach and, followed by the driver and guard, fled across the plain to the Pheasant Inn nearby. The lioness gave chase and knocked over one of the terrified passengers who, still shocked and bleeding, eventually made his way to the inn. The man never recovered and spent the last twenty-six years of his life in Laverstock mental asylum.

The Freeling Connection

Palmer had an equally worthy successor in Francis Freeling, whom he had met in Bath while researching his Plan for Reform. The two became friends and when Palmer was made Comptroller of the Mails, 21-year-old Freeling transferred with him to the General Post Office, where he worked as a surveyor. In 1792 Freeling was appointed head of the GPO's seven surveyors, touring the country and setting up penny posts in the main towns and cities. Five years later he was appointed joint post office secretary with Anthony Todd and, a year later, secretary in his own right. At that time, Sir William Pitt, the prime minister, often used the Post Office as a source of revenue – or a 'funding agency' as some people described it. At the start of the Napoleonic Wars in 1799, he repeatedly used Post Office finance to pay for armaments, ships and supplies and, to boost the coffers even further, he raised London's penny post to 2d for inner-city areas and 3d for outer London districts in 1801. Freeling liked Pitt and turned a blind eye to his manoeuvring. He was more interested in starting his own reform programme, moving the Post Office's Lombard Street headquarters, which now had three separate circulation departments – overseas, district and London mail – to a larger building with two distinctive doric pillars, at St Martin's-le-Grand, near St Paul's Cathedral. Freeling was also pleased to see that Pitt's new charges had not reduced London's postal volumes, and to give

Snow Coach. The elegant mail-coach was more vulnerable to heavy snowfalls than its chunky predecessor, and sometimes had to send urgent mail by horse rider after getting stuck in a drift

Emergency Stop. After attacking a horse of the Exeter mail-coach, this escaped lioness knocked over one of the fleeing passengers. The man never recovered and spent the rest of his life in a mental asylum

Pitt's Purge. The Tory prime minister Sir William Pitt often took money from the Post Office's coffers to pay for arms, ships and supplies during the Napoleonic Wars

customers value for money, he recruited teams of couriers to deliver the post to people's homes. Each day six open-sided 'Accelerator' omnibuses took the postmen from St Martin's-le-Grand to their London delivery rounds.

Soon the discovery of steam began to revolutionize postal travel. After successful trials with Stephenson's *Rocket* (see Chapter 9) and the opening of a railway link from Manchester to Liverpool in 1830, the Post Office started sending letters by steam train at the hitherto unheard of speed of 30 mph. Wishing to improve the overseas post, Freeling replaced the Post Office's sailing packet-boats with steam-powered ones. Finally the nineteenth-century reformer turned to crime prevention, issuing warning circulars and 'wanted' posters to help reduce money-letter thefts. Any postmaster or post-boy caught in the act was sent to prison (see Chapter 13), although until 1835 it had been a hanging offence. Freeling also introduced strict penalties for another crime that lost the Post Office valuable revenue – an illegal version of franking or forging MPs' signatures to qualify for free postage. Two of the most notorious frankers were the poets Coleridge and Shelley, who would often approach MPs and, pleading extreme poverty, persuade them to sign the backs of their letters. Shelley even forged his own MP father's signature. On one occasion Dr

Samuel Johnson gave his diarist James Boswell a letter to post, telling him: 'If such letters as this were to cost anything, I should hardly send them.'

The Poverty Trap

The roar of the industrial revolution was now being heard throughout Britain's factories and industrial towns. Britain had become the workshop of the world. However, 20 per cent of the population was living in poverty. And the sound of the postman's knock was one of dread to many a family, who often had to go out and sell a household item to pay for the postage on their letters.

All postal charges – apart from those in penny post cities – were still payable on receipt, each letter being taxed on the distance it had travelled and the number of sheets it held. Postal rates were high and continued to rise annually. In 1835 the cost of sending a one-sheet letter under 15 miles was 4*d*, up to 300 miles, 1*s*, plus 1*d* for every extra 100 miles travelled. Two-sheet and three-sheet letters cost double and triple, respectively, regardless of the number of miles covered. If a clerk was unsure of a letter's size, he used a method called candling – holding it against a lighted candle in a dark room – to find out the number of sheets it held. Most residents of large towns collected their

Black Marks. The writer Samuel Johnson often forged his postage, pointing out to his diarist James Boswell that he only sent letters because they didn't cost anything

Grand Master. Secretary Sir Francis Freeling moved the Post Office's headquarters from Lombard Street to a larger building at St Martin's-le-Grand

post from the nearest receiving-house, while those in smaller towns, villages and hamlets would pay the district postmaster or a local pauper to deliver it to them. The payment system was a complex one, and many receiving-houses employed several accountants to do their book-keeping.

As Britain's prosperity rose, so did her dependence on the postal system. More and more commercial firms were using the post for their transactions; pamphlets about school and university courses were regularly sent to parents; and the number of newspapers continued to grow. Businessmen and traders began to put pressure on the government to reduce postal rates, and in 1835, after a campaign led by Greenock MP, Robert Wallace, a government inquiry recommended cheaper postage and a streamlined delivery system. Freeling himself was an enthusiastic supporter of the campaign, but before he could start lobbying his government superiors, the 73-year-old reformer died during the night of 10 July 1836, at his home in London's Bryanston Square. He was later buried at St Mary Redcliffe church, Bristol, less than 200 yd from his birthplace.

It was left to a young civil servant named Rowland Hill to continue the campaign. In 1837 Hill produced a report 'Post Office Reform; Its Importance and Practicability' which contained a radical proposal – a penny for all British letters.

Postman's Knock. The arrival of the postman did not amuse members of poorer families when they had to go out and sell a household item to pay for postage

5

The Father of Invention

His great plan ran like wildfire through the civilised world.

William Gladstone

Rowland Hill spent much of his early career trying to avoid the poverty he had known as a child. With his brilliantly inventive mind, he was able to change jobs at will, each time improving both himself and his salary. He was a school-teacher at twelve, a headmaster at twenty-two, he followed a number of radical causes, worked with reformers like Robert Owen and Gibbon Wakefield, patented several inventions, and finally, at the age of thirty-nine, became a civil servant. Hill was quiet and studious, ungainly at sport, artistic, often ill, and despite his intellect, never went to university. Born at Kidderminster on 3 December 1795, he was one of a family of eight who according to a friend were 'preoccupied with making four pennies do as much as other families make fourpence halfpenny do'. His father, Thomas, was a man of great talent, but little resolve, working at many jobs – butcher's assistant, poncho maker, brass foundry manager and finally schoolmaster. Hill's mother, Sarah, was hardworking, courageous and dedicated. It was her inspiration that helped make him one of Britain's leading inventors and the Post Office's most successful reformer.

In 1803 Thomas Hill opened a school called Hill Top, where from an early age Hill was a pupil and teacher. The school was unique. Based on humanist principles, it had five main themes: voluntary learning; spare-time interests; moral training; the powers of reason; and kindness and consideration. Its ideas were later copied all over the world.

In 1818, when he was twenty-three, Hill designed a new school for the family. A square, sturdy, Queen Anne style building, it had such revolutionary features as airduct central heating, gaslights instead of candles, a library, small museum, craft room, science laboratory, stage, gymnasium, refectory and a study-block for the older boys, with an observatory and swimming pool in the school grounds. The school, Hazelwood, was opened in 1819.

Birth Mark. Rowland Hill's Kidderminster birthplace. After his death in 1867, a statue was erected outside the house

Three years later Hill and his brothers Matthew and Arthur produced a book, *Plans for the Government and Liberal Instruction of Boys in Large Numbers. Drawn from Experience*, which brought overnight fame to Hazelwood and was to have a profound influence on British education.

Apart from education, the idea of communications and the post office network appealed to Hill and he began to look at new ways to improve the post. In 1826 he devised a plan for sorting and date-stamping letters on mail-coaches, to help speed the mail – an idea that was realized in 1838 when the GPO introduced Travelling Post Offices on trains.

The following year the Hill brothers opened a new branch of the school called Bruce Castle in Tottenham, London. Soon after he was appointed headmaster, 32-year-old Hill married Caroline Pearson. He enjoyed his new role but his tendency to overwork had weakened his health and his salary was low. So he began to look for more lucrative posts. He had already considered forming self-help social communities with his brothers; he had also worked with the nineteenth-century reformer Robert Owen. But neither option offered good job prospects.

Instead, Hill settled for developing a range of inventions. In 1829 he devised a new pendulum that told the time by reflecting the stars, an idea supplanted by the invention of electricity. He then experimented with steam as a means of transport, until he found George Stephenson doing the same; he also carried out several dangerous and unsuccessful experiments with gunpowder.

Necessity is often the mother of invention, and with his brothers Frederic and Edwin and Professor Charles Wheatstone, one of the founders of the postal telegraph, Hill formed the Society for the Diffusion of Useful Knowledge (SDUK) – a sort of brains trust of inventors.

In 1830 Hill stumbled on his second postal invention when he discovered a way of carrying the mail by atmospheric pressure, a technique used by the GPO in 1863 when they opened an underground railway in London. Hill also drew up plans for a London coach company that could carry parcels and mail as well as passengers. And so the ideas kept coming: a pendulum for helping to drive steam engines, a screw for propelling steamboats, a new method of monitoring the speed of mail-coaches, ways of using piped gas, roadmaking equipment, and sending messages through tubes – later used by the GPO to send telegrams from the Telegraph Office to St Martin's-le-Grand.

One of Hill's outstanding inventions was the rotary press – the printing of newspapers in continuous rolls instead of single sheets. It could have revolutionized newspaper production in the 1830s, but the Treasury delayed it by insisting that all the sheets be separated and marked with a 1½d tax stamp before they went to press. As a result, the expansion of British newspapers was slower than it might have been.

In 1832 Hill published *Home Colonies: a Plan for the Gradual Extinction (by education) of Pauperism and the Diminution of Crime*, hoping it would attract enough attention to gain him a government job. The attempt failed. Instead, he became involved with the reformer Gibbon Wakefield, and from 1834 to 1839 worked as secretary to the South Australian Commission in London, helping Wakefield steer the South Australia Act through parliament.

While working at the Commission, Hill started a journal called *The Penny Magazine* with fellow SDUK member and publisher Charles Knight. But again his energetic mind turned to the Post Office, and in 1837 he produced a report 'Post Office Reform; Its Importance and Practicability', which he presented to the postmaster-general, Lord Lichfield. Lichfield showed little interest, so Hill published it in January 1837, and attracted considerable public support. A total of two hundred petitions with two hundred and fifty-five thousand signatories, including the Lord Mayor of London, were presented to parliament.

Master Plan. Forty-year-old Rowland Hill was working as a civil servant at the South Australian Commission in London when he devised his plan for a penny post

In his report, Hill called for a fair and practical postal system; not a money-making commercial venture. He pointed out that postal rates had soared above most people's means and should be reduced to 1*d* per letter. Hill's analysis was simple. Each letter cost only a fraction of a penny to deliver, whether going to Scotland or a local town, as the overheads – sorting and stamping, mail-coach maintenance, and the wages of the driver and guard – were the same for every item whether travelling 500 or 2 miles.

As an economist, Hill disliked a system that gave free postage to MPs and prominent people, and cost the Post Office a considerable amount of potential income. His other *bête noire* was the multi-purpose letter when senders put several letters on one sheet, which was then cut up by the recipient and delivered to a number of people in the same area – all for the price of one letter.

The Hill philosophy was that all letters should be prepaid. The existing method of payment on receipt was expensive and time-wasting. Addressees were often out when the postman called, and he often had to wait more than an hour for them to return, or else go back another day to collect the money. There was also the dilemma of the addressees who could not afford to pay for their letters. Hill had never forgotten his mother's anxiety when a letter with a high postal duty was delivered, nor the time when she sent him out to sell a bag of clothes to raise 3*s* for a batch of letters. Another victim of payment on delivery was the postman. Often he had to carry large amounts of money, making him an easy target for robbers and accidents.

Neither the government nor the Post Office were convinced by the Hill formula. So he put his theories to the test. A group of postmen were sent out on a daily round, some carrying prepaid letters, the others collecting the money. It was found that those carrying prepaid letters could deliver five hundred in half-an-hour, while the collectors were delivering about sixty-seven letters in one-and-a-half hours. Hill's argument was unshakeable. It was also supported by the founder of the campaign for cheaper post, MP Robert Wallace (see Chapter 4), and *The Times*, which ran a series of persuasive leaders. Finally, a group of London merchants and bankers formed the Mercantile Committee, which promoted the Hill formula in a series of penetrating newspaper articles and petitions.

Though a government inquiry had been looking into the Post Office since 1835, it had only produced a few mild recommendations like the need for competitive tenders for mail-coaches, a more efficiently run overseas packet service and the introduction of registered letters, as well as some vaguely phrased sentiments about the need to reduce postal charges and improve standards of delivery. When Hill was eventually summoned to the inquiry on 13 February 1837, he proposed another ingenious idea – envelopes for letter-carrying – adding that:

> Perhaps this idea might be obviated by using a bit of paper . . . and covered at the back with a glutinous wash, which the bringer might, by the application of a little moisture, attach to the back of the letter.

He was not only proposing envelopes but postage stamps. Again the government and Post Office were indifferent.

However, because of public pressure, the government set up a select committee. The Post Office secretary Colonel William Maberly told the committee that Hill's ideas were 'fallacious, preposterous, utterly unsupported by facts and resting entirely upon assumptions', adding that the Post Office would take fifty years to recover from such loss-making lunacy. While the postmaster-general, Lord Lichfield, commented: 'Of all the wild and visionary schemes I have heard of, this is the most extraordinary.' And a third Post Office manager said Hill's report was 'a meddling form of quackery'.

The select committee was adamant that all letters should continue to be paid on a collect basis, those weighing up to half an ounce costing 2d, with an extra 1d for each additional ounce. But, not to be outdone, the determined Mercantile Committee continued its Penny Post campaign. Fearing for their election prospects, the Whig government passed the Penny Postage Act in August 1839. The Duke of Wellington, leader of the Tory opposition, the Penny Post's severest critic, said the Act had been passed 'with great reluctance and pain'.

The following month the Treasury offered Hill a two year contract and a £500 a year salary to run the new system. Unhappy with such a meagre sum, Hill turned it down. The Treasury then raised it to £1,500 a year and Hill accepted. His assistant for the two year project was Henry Cole, founder of the Mercantile Committee.

In December 1839, when the Act became law, the man in the street could be forgiven for throwing his best hat into the River Thames in disgust. For, apart

UNIFORM PENNY POSTAGE.

A Public Meeting

Of the Bankers, Merchants, & Traders, of the City of London,

WILL BE HELD AT THE

EGYPTIAN HALL OF THE MANSION HOUSE,

ON

Wednesday Next, July 10,

To Petition Parliament for the Adoption of Mr. ROWLAND HILL'S *Plan of a* UNIFORM PENNY POSTAGE,

AS RECOMMENDED BY THE SELECT

Committee of the House of Commons.

THE RIGHT HON. THE LORD MAYOR,

Will take the Chair at TWO o'Clock precisely.

The Metropolitan Members are expected to attend.

PRINTED BY T. BRETTELL, RUPERT STREET, HAYMARKET.

Campaign Call. The Mercantile Committee of merchants and bankers issued many propaganda posters before the Penny Post became law

from abolishing free franking for MPs and VIPs, it said the penny rate should only apply to London and the existing penny post cities, introducing a fourpenny post for the rest of the country. A political compromise if ever there was one, and the public reacted with a cascade of petitions, letters and demonstrations. Then, to everyone's relief, on 10 January 1840, the Whig government introduced a penny rate for all British letters under half an ounce and said all post should be prepaid. The Penny Post had made its entrance at last.

The first letter of the new post was sent by Samuel Lines, Rowland Hill's former art teacher who lived in Birmingham. Lines wrote to congratulate Hill on the success of his new reforms on 9 January, taking the letter to Birmingham's main post office. At a minute after midnight on 10 January he banged on the door until a rather startled postal clerk came and collected it. Lines' letter was one of a hundred and twelve thousand penny post letters sent throughout Britain that day – three times the national average.

Nearly everyone who could read and write was now able to afford to send a letter. The Post Office had become a public institution and no longer a slightly eccentric network served by a motley collection of post-boys and robber-proof carts. But the British public were to be treated to yet another of Hill's surprise packages.

For the next few months, senders continued to pay a local postal clerk each time they sent a letter. Then in April 1840, Hill and Cole ran a competition with a first prize of £200 to find the best way to prepay letters. It attracted two thousand six hundred entries, but not one of them was considered suitable. So Hill decided to adopt two of his own ideas. The first was an envelope with a picture of Britannia and her trident surrounded by members of her colonies drawn by the nineteenth-century artist William Mulready. The second was a postage stamp, known as a Penny Black, showing a portrait of Queen Victoria and designed by William Wyon of the Royal Mint.

Both ideas were adopted by the Post Office on 6 May 1840.

That year postal volumes doubled to 140 million items, tripling the following year to 208 million. However, the Penny Post still had its Post Office critics who described penny blacks as 'government sticking-plasters' and said it was better to have an expensive service with fewer items than a low-cost one with more, while the Mulready envelope's picture of Britannia

Sticking Plaster. The world's first stamp, the Penny Black, was described as a 'government sticking-plaster' by its critics

Last Laugh. The Mulready envelope, showing Britannia with her colonial subjects, was greeted with such mirth that it had to be withdrawn

was greeted with such mirth by the general public and London's cartoonists that it was withdrawn in 1841 and replaced by a plain white envelope.

Hill appointed his elder brother, Edwin, to run the Stamp Office, and together they produced a successor to the Penny Black, the Twopenny Blue, which was used for overseas mail. After experimenting with different dyes, Edwin Hill produced a reddish-brown version of the Penny Black in 1841, called the Penny Red. The postage stamp was here to stay. By 1854 twenty-one countries were producing their own multi-coloured versions.

Hill's initiative was not without its faults. At the end of his two year term he was startled to find that although postal volumes had increased, revenues had not. In fact it took ten years for the new penny and twopenny rates to raise Post Office turnover and another thirty to increase profits. However, the Penny Post had succeeded in bringing postage within everyone's reach and putting the private carriers out of business. Nonetheless the radical Hill faced the hostility of Colonel Maberly and the Post Office's old guard, and in 1843 the Tory prime minister Sir Robert Peel decided not to renew Hill's two year Post Office contract.

Hill's First Goodbye

It looked like Hill's Post Office epitaph and he began looking for alternative employment. As a young man, Hill had been intrigued by the steam locomotive, devising several ideas for improving it. Impressed by the reformer's early prowess, the owners of the London and Brighton Railway Company, which had fallen into debt and badly needed reorganizing, asked him to be their director. Hill duly obliged.

Within months he had put the company back into profit, monitoring locomotives' punctuality by riding at the front with a stop-watch. After being promoted to company chairman, Hill introduced the first cheap excursions to the seaside for those who could not afford rail fares or holidays.

Farewell Gesture. When Rowland Hill was dismissed by the Tories in 1843, *Punch* published a cartoon of Britannia presenting him with a postman's sack

Meanwhile back at Hill's alma mater, a total of six hundred and twenty new rural deliveries were now serving nineteen hundred British villages, and there were changes at St Martin's-le-Grand. However, the loyal British public had not forgotten Hill and in June 1846 a fund was started which raised more than £13,000 in tribute to Hill and his reforms. Soon afterwards, the Whigs returned to power and offered Hill a second spell at the Post Office. This time it was to be an official post.

Hill had been hoping to succeed Maberly as Post Office Secretary, the equivalent of chief executive, but he was offered the subordinate post of Secretary to the Postmaster-General and a salary of £1,200. Slightly reluctantly he accepted, and found most of his decisions had to be approved by the reactionary Maberly. Yet Hill was a fine advocate and a hard man to refuse, and his next eight years proved to be his most fertile. Despite suffering bouts of his childhood asthma, 51-year-old Hill set about his new task with gusto.

His first reform was innocent enough. In 1848 Hill introduced a Book Post, which reduced the high fees library book borrowers had to pay when returning books by post. His next measure, however, was far more controversial. He introduced Sunday sorting at St Martin's-le-Grand to ensure mail was forwarded to the provinces early in the week. Soon he was facing vigorous opposition from the Lord's Day Observance Society, who organized demonstrations and banner-waving marches through London over what they considered a flagrant breach of the day of rest. As a result, Hill had to make Sunday working voluntary instead of compulsory.

Hill's other measures were more universal. To make deliveries easier, he appealed to members of the public to put up their own street or garden post-boxes, or else to cut slots in their front-doors; he also supported a plan of the novelist Anthony Trollope, a surveyor in the West Country, to widen postal distribution by putting up pillar-boxes. As a result six boxes were erected in London in 1855. Both ideas had originated from the French postal service.

A Family Business

In 1850 Hill's son Pearson joined the Post Office as Colonel Maberly's junior clerk. Pearson had inherited many of his father's talents and, over the next few years, introduced two postal innovations – mechanical lifts for loading and unloading mail from Travelling Post Offices, and a date-stamping and

By Command of the Postmaster General.

NOTICE to the PUBLIC.

Rapid Delivery of Letters.

GENERAL POST OFFICE,
May, 1849.

The Postmaster General is desirous of calling attention to the greater rapidity of delivery which would obviously be consequent on the general adoption of *Street-door Letter Boxes, or Slits,* in private dwelling houses, and indeed wherever the Postman is at present kept waiting.

He hopes that householders will not object to the means by which, at a very moderate expense, they may secure so desirable an advantage to themselves, to their neighbours, and to the Public Service.

Personal Touch. The Post Office asked members of the public to put up street-door letter-boxes or to make slits in their front doors to ease letter delivery

cancelling machine that was still in use at the start of the twentieth century. In 1851 Rowland Hill's youngest brother Frederic became his assistant, and together they increased the number of postmen, opened new rural posts and supervised the building of town and country post offices. When Maberly was moved sideways to another civil service position three year later, Hill became Post Office Secretary, while his brother was appointed joint assistant secretary with responsibility for the Money Order and Overseas Mail Packets offices. Hill's other assistant secretary was Anthony Trollope's brother-in-law John Tilley.

He continued his reform programme, merging London's General and District postmen and opening a new distribution department at St Martin's-le-Grand. He also carried out his earlier pledge to merge the overseas, provincial and London divisions into one circulation department. Lastly Hill recruited women to work in clerical posts, a move that was more economic than emancipated as women were paid lower wages than men.

In London, which handled a quarter of the country's correspondence, he reintroduced twelve deliveries a day – every hour, and on the hour – and divided the capital into ten separate 'towns' with their own sorting-offices and postmen, to prevent congestion. The new system responded so quickly to Hill's touch that by 1857, 65 per cent of London's mail was being delivered before 9 a.m. Meanwhile, thanks to Hill and his brother Frederic, British villagers and townsfolk were enjoying the fruits of the penny post as more and more postmen began to trudge the country lanes and streets and handy post-boxes popped up to take the letters.

Brother Frederic had been hard at work on his own projects, too. After introducing the first Post Office annual reports, he started a life insurance scheme and widows and orphans fund – the Rowland Hill Benevolent Fund – for postal employees and their families. He then converted parts of St Martin's-le-Grand into new sorting and collection areas.

Though postmen had won a place in British people's hearts, Hill was dissatisfied with the way they were recruited. Most postal employees were nominated for their jobs by local MPs or dignitaries, which struck Hill as wasteful and élitist. In 1854 he published a report recommending competitive examinations for clerks, sorters and postmen, including those recommended by 'influential friends'. The report was adopted by the government and within five years nearly all the Post Office's 25,000-strong workforce were taking entry exams. One advertisement in *The Times* for twenty-two letter-carriers attracted twelve hundred applicants.

By 1859 more than 90 per cent of British letters were being delivered prepaid, and most towns and cities outside London were getting a regular three deliveries a day. Hill had made his point, and on the Penny Post's twentieth anniversary in 1860, he was knighted by Queen Victoria.

A grateful British public began to wonder if, in the words of Sir Francis Freeling, 'the wonderful improvements with which the present age abounds' would ever cease. Hill soon gave them an answer. In 1861 a banker named Charles W. Sikes noticed that many poorer people were finding it difficult to open bank accounts, for nineteenth-century savings banks were only interested in customers with large sums of money to deposit. So he approached Hill with the idea of setting up Post Office savings banks. Hill took to it at once and soon savings banks were installed at all the main post offices. The new investors were allowed to save up to £30 a year and hold a maximum of £150, though the limits were later raised. One of the scheme's supporters was Whig prime minister William Gladstone who said that the savings banks promoted 'self-help and thrift among the working classes'. Perhaps the only radical idea Rowland Hill failed to introduce during his secretaryship was a cheap parcel

Saving Grace. One of the supporters of post
office savings banks was Whig premier
William Gladstone who said they promoted
'self-help and thrift among the working-classes'

post to compete with the high rates of private carriers, though it was adopted in 1885. However, in 1863 Frederic Hill persuaded the Treasury to introduce a cheap rate Pattern Post for traders who wanted to send samples through the post.

Hill's Second Goodbye

Now aged sixty-nine and suffering repeated bouts of ill health, Hill decided to retire in March 1864 – and the tributes flowed in. The Treasury said:

> The postal system, one of the most powerful organs which modern civilisation has placed at the command of Government, has, mainly under the auspices and by the agency of Sir Rowland Hill, been, within the last quarter of a century, not merely improved but transformed. The letters transmitted have increased nearly ninefold, and have been carried at what may be estimated as little more than one-ninth of the former charge.

Gladstone commented that: 'He stands pre-eminent and alone among all the members of the civil service as a benefactor to the Nation. His great plan ran like wildfire through the civilized world.' Hill was also given a 'thank-you' gift of £20,000 and his full salary as a pension for life. Other honours followed – the Society of Arts Albert Gold Medal, an honorary doctorate of law at Oxford University, the Freedom of the City of London, and Fellowship of the Royal Society for Hill's early discoveries in astronomy.

His last act of public service was with the government's Royal Commission on Railways between 1865 and 1867. He then spent the rest of his retirement going for long walks with his wife, Caroline, near their Hampstead Heath home, visiting the occasional meeting of London's Political Economy Club and working on his autobiography with his nephew, George.

After further ill health, Hill died at home on 27 August 1879. A state memorial service was held at Westminster Abbey on 4 September, when, as a last tribute, all the London shops were closed for the day. The two hour service was attended by more than six hundred people including Hill's successor at the Post Office, Sir John Tilley, the Lord Mayor of London, the Astronomer-Royal, MPs, writers, artists, inventors, and many of Hill's Post Office

SIR ROWLAND LE GRAND.

Grand Finale. A *Punch* cartoon showing Sir Rowland Hill being presented with a laurel wreath on his retirement. The caption said: 'Should Rowland Hill have a statue? Certainly, if Oliver Cromwell should. For one is celebrated for cutting off the head of a bad Queen, and the other for sticking on the head of a good Queen.'

contemporaries. Hill was buried at St Paul's Chapel, a few feet away from another contemporary, James Watt, the discoverer of steam power. Later two statues were erected in Hill's memory at his Kidderminster birthplace and outside St Martin's-le-Grand.

Perhaps the great reformer's most fitting epitaph was uttered by his brother Matthew who told him one day:

> When you go to Heaven, I foresee that you will stop at the gate to enquire of St Peter how many deliveries they have a day, and how the postal communication between Heaven and the other place is defrayed.

6

A Man of Letters

The pillar-box . . . an object full of civic dignity, the treasure-house of a
thousand secrets, the fortunes of a thousand souls . . . there it stands at all
our street corners, disguising one of the most beautiful ideas under one of
the most preposterous of forms.

G.K. Chesterton

Anthony Trollope's childhood was as bizarre and unexpected as the plots of
many of his novels. His father Thomas, a Fellow of New College, Oxford, was
a barrister who, tiring of the dry, legal world, became a gentleman-farmer.
However, instead of farming, he spent most of the time writing an
encyclopedia of the church, and one farm after another had to close due to lack
of care and profit. In some ways Trollope's childhoood resembled that of
Rowland Hill's – a constant struggle against poverty. Trollope's mother,
Frances, was pretty, artistic, and sociable and while he was a boy she went to
America to open a shop and start a writing career to salvage some of the
family's income and pride. Anthony Trollope was born on 24 April 1815, in
Keppel Street, off Russell Square, London, not far from his father's legal
chambers at Lincoln's Inn. Though an eloquent lawyer, Thomas Trollope had a
fiery temper, which tended to drive his fellow attorneys away, and often his
clients as well. As a result, he moved from one set of dingy chambers to the
next.

While he was still a baby, Trollope's parents moved to Julians Farm in
Harrow-on-the-Hill, where Thomas Trollope built a new house on the basis of
a promised inheritance from his uncle. However, when the uncle remarried, he
changed his will and Thomas Trollope received nothing. Soon he found
himself in financial straits. Though he had been a successful lawyer with a
sizeable income, most of his capital had been spent on building the house. As a
last resort he let the house to tenants to raise money, moving his family to
another Harrow farm and returning to his legal practice. Trollope, who was
now seven, was sent to Harrow School, where he spent three miserable years

Dual Role. Anthony Trollope combined an impressive postal career with novel-writing. 'I had thought very much more about the Post Office than I had of my literary work,' he wrote in his autobiography

before his parents despatched him to a school run by a family friend at Sunbury-on-Thames, Surrey. Again Trollope was unhappy. Because of his ungainly appearance he was frequently bullied, and his schoolwork suffered as well. All was not well with Thomas Trollope either. His health was failing and he was becoming reclusive, spending more and more time on his history of the church amd less on his legal work. With six children and a wife to support, he was beginning to find his daily tasks increasingly burdensome. His only option was to search for new sources of income. Eventually, the Trollopes decided that Frances should go to America with their son, Henry, and his two sisters to seek an alternative living.

Anthony, then aged twelve, was sent to his father's old school, Winchester College, where his elder brother, Thomas Adolphus, was also a pupil. One of the school's traditions was that an older brother should act as his younger brother's tutor. Duties included character-building, and each day Thomas Adolphus had to beat his brother with a large stick. Meanwhile the trials of Thomas Trollope continued. His health had got so bad that he had to retire from the Bar, he had no capital left, and his foolhardy dream of becoming a gentleman-farmer still lingered. Despite his ignorance of farming methods, he took a lease on another farm, employing several farm-hands to help him. Thomas struggled to succeed for eighteen months, then abandoned the idea altogether and set off with Thomas Adolphus to Cincinnati, Ohio, where his wife had opened a shop selling small household goods.

While his parents were away, a new fate awaited Trollope. As his father had failed to pay his college bills, the school tradesmen refused to give him credit and he was unable to wear his school uniform. With his ungainly, and now dishevelled appearance, he became an even more obvious target for the bullies. The desperate Trollope even pondered 'whether I could not find my way up to the top of that college tower, and from thence put an end to everything'. Then suddenly Trollope thought he had found merciful release. His father, who had been unable to settle in America, came back to England and, saddened by his son's plight, sent him back to Harrow as a day pupil. The fifteen-year-old Trollope had a round trip of 12 miles to and from school each day, made no new friends and found that the farmhouse where he and his father lived 'seemed always to be in danger of falling into the neighbouring horse-pond'. He later described this period as the worst of his life. 'What right had a wretched farmer's boy, reeking from a dunghill, to sit next to the sons of peers – or much worse still, next to the sons of big tradesmen who had made their ten-thousand a year?' he wrote in his autobiography. One day, unable to bear the humiliation any longer, he picked a fight with a fellow pupil and hurt him badly. However, instead of feeling remorse, Trollope was triumphant. He was a winner at last and could hold his head a little higher. Meanwhile, Thomas Trollope's fortunes continued to falter. He owed money to his landlord and all the local tradesmen and was feeling so poorly that he had to spend half the time in bed. Nevertheless, while he was shaving each morning at 6.00 a.m., he would make Trollope stand next to him and recite his Latin and Greek rules and grammar. However, this early grounding had little effect on his son. Trollope later recalled: 'I look back on my resolute idleness and fixed determination to make no use whatever of the books thrust upon me.'

Trollope the Penniless Postal Worker

In 1831, when Trollope was sixteen, Frances returned to England with a book she had just finished, called *Domestic Manners of the Americans*. She approached several publishers before a London firm agreed to take it. When the book was published it was an immediate success, which meant the Trollope family could move into the house that Thomas had originally built and enjoy some home comforts for the first time.

Young Anthony was still suffering at Harrow. Day pupils were not allowed to join societies or play games; he therefore spent most of his spare time reading and re-reading the first two volumes of J. Fennimore Cooper's *The Prairie*. Trollope also showed little interest in his studies. He sat for several scholarships to Oxford and Cambridge, but failed all of them. Thus his parents had to abandon their hopes of a free university education, and at the age of nineteen, he left Harrow with no qualifications and a poor grasp of Latin and Greek. Apart from the Law, medicine, the Church and the armed forces there were few jobs for upper-middle-class 'gentlemen'. The alternative was the civil service. Frances Trollope was friendly with the daughter-in-law of Post Office secretary Francis Freeling and managed to arrange an 'interview' for Trollope. In those days of patronage and influential friends, an interview was as good as a job offer, and in 1834 Trollope was asked if he would like to work as a junior clerk in Francis Freeling's department.

Trollope's interview resembled a scene in one of his satirical novels.

> When I got to the 'Grand', as we would call our office in those days, from its site in St Martin's-le-Grand, I was seated at a desk without any further reference to my competency. No-one condescended even to look at my beautiful penmanship. That was the way in which candidates for the civil service were interviewed in my young days.

He took the job and its annual salary of £90, on which he managed to find some spartan-looking digs in central London. Still somewhat odd in appearance with a large head and long blond curly hair, Trollope had a generous personality and ready wit and made friends easily. With two of his colleagues he formed a walking club called The Tramp Society, and on the evenings and weekends when he wasn't drinking and playing poker, he and his friends explored the towns around London and lesser-known parts of the home counties.

At work, Trollope formed a close friendship with Sir Francis Freeling. The Post Office secretary wrote Trollope long, lucid notes on all aspects of postal life on which he would ask him to comment. Trollope, in turn, would often use them to prepare his own departmental reports. Some of these notes, which have only recently been discovered and renamed 'The Freeling Papers', give a fascinating insight into the workings of the nineteenth-century Post Office. They undoubtedly helped Trollope form his own highly individual style, so that he could discard the classical refinements of public school English and write openly, humorously and satirically.

A year after Trollope joined the Post Office, Sir Francis Freeling fell ill and was confined to his sick-bed, but he still continued to send Trollope little notes until his death in 1837. Trollope had lost a very good friend, and his successor Colonel Maberly, a stern, unforgiving traditionalist, was a very different character.

> He was certainly not my friend . . . it was not considered to be much in
> my favour that I could write letters – which was mainly the work of our
> office – rapidly, correctly, and to the purpose.

One incident in particular made an indelible blot on Trollope's career. Each morning he would take Maberly's mail into the secretary's office. Maberly would then open the letters, and start composing suitable replies. However, one day he opened one to find it full of bank-notes. Leaving the letter on his desk, he went out of the room, only for Trollope to return a few minutes later to finish some of his own paperwork. After about five minutes, Colonel Maberly also returned. The letter and the money had disappeared. He immediately sent for Trollope shouting, 'The letter has been taken, and, by God! there has been nobody in the room but you and I', and hammering his fist on the desk. Trollope shouted back, 'Then, by God! you have taken it,' and he too slammed his fist down on Maberly's desk, upsetting a bottle of ink and spattering Maberly's face and shirt front. Seething with anger, the red-faced colonel leapt up and was about to punch Trollope in the stomach when his private secretary ran into the room with the missing money-letter. The relationship between Maberly and Trollope never recovered.

Trouble of all kinds seemed to seek out young Trollope. A woman he had met in a country village one day wanted to marry him, writing him a succession of letters claiming she was about to have his child, all of which Trollope ignored. Then an older woman arrived at St Martin's-le-Grand 'with a large basket on her arm and an immense bonnet on her head'. It was the girl's mother, and walking up the middle of the huge room Trollope shared with six postal clerks, she announced in a loud voice: 'Anthony Trollope, when are you going to marry my daughter?' Trollope replied, 'I never intend to marry your daughter', and somehow managed to calm the woman down. He never heard from the mother or her daughter again.

Trollope found Post Office routine irksome, referring to his first seven years as 'neither creditable to myself nor useful to the public service'. He always arrived at the 'Grand' ten minutes late and left at exactly 4.30 each afternoon, sometimes leaving his work unfinished which did not endear him to his managers. As he went about his duties, the young postal clerk created many of his plots – 'I was always going about with some castle in the air' – while his colleagues provided him with several useful character studies for his novels.

Permanently haunted by poverty, Trollope was followed to work for several months by a money-lender with a starched white cravate. Occasionally the money-lender would appear during the day and follow him home, like a walking shadow. Eventually Trollope gave him some money, and he disappeared as fleetingly as he had appeared. Though his mother sometimes baled him out, Trollope was never able to afford more than a few basic necessities and spent many hours reading in his lonely room.

Writing books seemed an obvious way out of his demise.

I had thought it possible that I might write a novel. I had resolved very early that in that shape must the attempt be made. But the months and years ran on, and no attempt was made. And yet no day was passed without thoughts of attempting, and a mental acknowledgement of the disgrace of postponing, it.

In 1841, a year after Rowland Hill's Penny Post, Trollope saw an advertisement at the 'Grand' for a surveyor's clerk in the west of Ireland. The job appealed to him and he duly applied. To his surprise, he received a letter back a week later offering him the post. It was an offer he could not refuse. Trollope's present salary was only £140. The new posting was worth £400, plus bonuses and mobility allowance. Though his relatives and friends were doubtful as Ireland had a reputation for poverty and hardship, Trollope was determined. He was unhappy with his London life and his father had recently died. It was time for a change.

Road Weary. A slightly scruffy post-boy delivers a batch of letters at the end of a long and tiring journey

Trollope the Trouble-Shooter

When he arrived at the little Irish town of Banagher on the River Shannon, 26-year-old Trollope saw an enchanting landscape of open fields, hills and valleys. Venturing into the town, he found his new office and met his new boss, the local surveyor, who told him that his job was to investigate complaints about the postal service. Trollope decided to travel the area on horseback, a habit he had enjoyed ever since he went on hunting expeditions with his father. Fortunately, the surveyor was a lazy man who seldom bothered to check on his employees' activities, which meant Trollope was often able to combine his postal duties with an afternoon's hunting in a 'land flowing with fun and whisky, in which irregularity was the rule of life' and where the people were 'good-humoured, clever, economical, and hospitable'.

As he rode the hills and dales, solving problems and meeting new customers, Trollope was more like a troubleshooter than a clerk, his only real work being to write up an activities report at the end of the day. After a year, the Irish surveyor told head office that Trollope was a most capable public servant, in refreshing contrast to Colonel Maberly's assessment of him as 'a very bad worker'.

Trollope spent three years on Ireland's west coast, spending his days off hunting or walking by the River Shannon. One day, while visiting a pub in the small town of Kingsdown, a pretty girl caught his eye. Introducing himself, they starting chatting and he found out that her name was Rose Heseltine and that she was the daughter of a bank manager in Rotherham, Yorkshire. As she was staying with some local relatives, they started courting.

Now love as well as hunting, Irish whiskey, and the vibrant Irish air were distracting Trollope from his ambition to write. When visiting counties like Cork, Kerry and Clare, Trollope saw the 'terrible evil of poverty' that had been caused by a succession of bad harvests, and during the summer of 1844, while he and a Tramp Society colleague, John Merivale, were exploring the little village of Drumsna they came upon the ruins of a country house. As they looked over its crumbling walls and decaying wooden beams, a mood of melancholy overcame them. Suddenly Trollope took out a pen and started to write – and continued to do so for almost two days. The inspiration had begun to flow at last. Soon he had finished the first chapter of a novel.

Two months later he and Rose travelled to England where they were married in Rose's home town of Rotherham. On their return, they were thrilled to discover that Trollope had been promoted to postal surveyor for southern Ireland. It meant that he and Rose were able to rent a house in the fashionable town of Clonmel, where, as well as his new postal duties, Trollope was able to spend the next few months continuing his novel. He finished *The Macdermotts of Ballydoran*, about Ireland before and after the famine, in 1845, sending the first draft to his mother, Frances, now a successful author. She liked it and arranged to have the book published by her own publishers. Encouraged by his first effort, Trollope wrote another called *The Kellys and the O'Kellys*, also about Ireland, which was published in 1848.

Neither book sold well, though *The Kellys* was given a review in *The Times*. But these two achievements made Trollope even more determined to succeed as a writer. He travelled to London, and using his flair for business and negotiation, secured a £20 advance for a third novel, *La Vendee*. However when it was published in 1850, only a few copies managed to sell. So the fledgling writer decided to turn his hand to playwriting, which he did not find easy. However, he was also commissioned by the famous nineteenth-century publisher John Murray, to write a guide to Ireland, after which he was asked to write a series of articles in the contemporary Liberal newspaper, *The Examiner*, about Ireland's current plight.

Trollope the Traveller

In 1851 Trollope began a special project to extend British letter-deliveries. For the first few months he helped improve Irish deliveries before plying his trade in the West Country, Wales and the Channel Islands, a phase he described as 'probably the happiest two years of my life'.

During his travels, Trollope discovered a haphazard network of delays, misrouting, overlapping and neglect by letter-carriers. So each day he would travel about 50 miles on horseback, accompanied by his faithful Irish groom, finding out how letters were being delivered, at what hour of the day, and whether customers were being charged, which was now forbidden. He found some couriers were illegally charging a penny for delivery, alleging the house they were visiting was off their normal beat, while influential home-owners were bribing couriers to deliver letters for them. Trollope sought out the culprit couriers and charged them 5s apiece.

Trollope would often ride with the couriers, in between bouts of hunting, showing them the best routes and short-cuts on a large map. One young householder recalls a visit from Trollope:

> The stranger, I can just recollect, as I watched him at our midday dinner, seemingly added to his naturally large dimensions by a shaggy overcoat, or it may have been a large, double-breasted pea jacket, making him look like one of those sea-captains about whom in the 1850s we used to hear a great deal on the Devonshire coast.

He rapidly raised the number of deliveries until most remote areas in the West Country had more than six posts a week. Like Rowland Hill, Trollope's ambition was to cover the whole of Britain with postmen. He says proudly in his autobiography:

> It is amusing how a passion will grow upon a man. I was a beneficent angel to the public, bringing everywhere with me an earlier, cheaper and much more regular delivery of letters . . . and I believe that many a farmer now has his letters brought daily to his house free of charge, who but for me would still have had to send to the post-town for them twice a week, or to have paid a man for bringing them irregularly to his door.

Pillars of the Community

One day, while visiting St Helier, the capital of Jersey, Trollope noticed a marked lack of postal services. Suddenly an idea sprang to him. During a short trip to France he had seen iron-stumps being used as roadside post-boxes, and he wrote to the Post Office's Eastern England surveyor, George Cresswell:

> There is, at present, no receiving-office in St Helier, and persons living in the distant parts of the town have to send nearly a mile to the principal office. I believe that a plan has obtained in France of fitting up letter-boxes in posts fixed at the roadside, and it may perhaps be thought advisable to try the operation of this system in St Helier – postage stamps are sold in every street and, therefore, all that is wanted is a safe receptacle for letters . . . iron posts suited for the purpose may be erected at the corners of streets in such situations as may be desirable, or probably it may be found more serviceable to fix iron letter boxes about 5 feet from the ground, wherever permanently

built walls, fit for the purpose, can be found, and I think that the public may safely be invited to use such boxes for depositing their letters. . . .

Cresswell forwarded Trollope's letter to St Martin's-le-Grand. A month later they wrote back agreeing to a trial run of seven boxes, four in Jersey and three in Guernsey. Meanwhile a local blacksmith, John Vaudin, of Le Feuvre's Foundry, St Helier, set to work to make the cast-iron pillars. The first four went up in St Helier in 1852, and within days, local residents were paying visits to their nearest post-box to post their letters or simply admire John Vaudin's handiwork (one of his boxes is still in use in the town). The enthusiastic St Helier postmaster wrote to St Martin's-le-Grand, 'More and more post-boxes must be introduced liberally and energetically'.

The first English post-box was erected at Butchergate, Carlisle, in September 1853, and on 11 April 1955 six were introduced in London. The

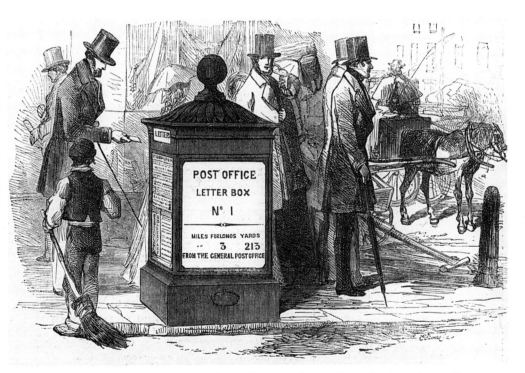

Street Wise. The public were delighted when they found they could post their letters in roadside pillar-boxes. Here is the first London box at the junction of Farringdon Street and Fleet Street

ROAD-SIDE
LETTER BOXES.

Notice to the Public.

On and after the 23rd Nov., Road-side Letter Boxes will be opened for collecting the public corespondence in the following situations :—

DAVID PLACE,
Nearly opposite the Rectory.

NEW STREET,
In front of Mr. Ivry's, Painter and Glazier.

CHEAPSIDE,
Top of the Parade.

ST. CLEMENT's ROAD,
Corner of Plaisance.

The Letter Boxes will be cleared daily (Sundays excepted) at the following periods, until further notice :

SIX A. M. AND AT NOON,

Except on Mail-days, when, instead of at Noon, they will be cleared as soon as the Packet is signalled.

Letters deposited in these Boxes will be disposed of in all respects in the same manner as if posted at the Principal Office, previous to the above-named period.

Post-office, St. Helier, November, 1852.

PRINTED AT "THE JERSEY TIMES" OFFICE, LIBRARY-PLACE.

Box Clever. A notice introducing the first pillar-boxes at St Helier, Jersey, in 1852

first, which bore the inscription 'Letter-Box Number 1' was installed at the corner of Fleet Street and Farringdon Street; the second was put up on the south side of The Strand, followed by four more in Pall Mall, Piccadilly, Grosvenor Place and Rutland Gate.

Later Trollope introduced one in his novel *He Knew He Was Right* when the character Jemima Stanbury said she

> had not the faintest belief that any letter put into one of them would ever reach its destination. She could not understand why people should not walk with their letters to a respectable post-office instead of chucking them into an iron-stump . . . out in the middle of the street with nobody to look after it. Positive orders were given that no letters from her house should ever be put into the iron post.

Trollope had more than fulfilled his letter-delivery contract. 'I should have liked to ride over the whole country, and to have sent a rural post letter-carrier to every parish, every village, every hamlet, and every grange in England,' he said. But the two-year project had one drawback. It had left him with little time for the writer's gift of contemplation.

One day in 1852, while gazing at the spire of Salisbury Cathedral, he was struck by an idea for a novel about the Church and its injustices. Again work intervened. Trollope was promoted to Northern Ireland surveyor with an annual salary of £800. So he and Rose and their two baby sons moved to a house in Belfast, Trollope spending the next few months getting to know the area, meeting local postmasters and their clerks and studying ways to improve the Northern Ireland post. At the end of the year, he started writing his novel about the Church and finished it in a year. When *The Warden*, first of the Barchester Chronicles, was published in 1855, it had a creditable reception, and Trollope was able to keep half the book's profits.

Pleased with *The Warden*'s success, Trollope got involved in some more journalism, publishing two articles, on Julius Caesar and Emperor Augustus, in the Dublin University magazine. However, when Trollope asked for payment, the editor told him that the honour of writing for his magazine more than made up for any payment.

Roadside boxes have appeared in many guises: a. A Parisian box of 1850; b. A Victorian box at Banbury, near Oxford; c. A torpedo-shaped box that stood in Aberdeen until 1956; d. A flood-proof box designed by the Department of Science and Art in 1857; e. A streamlined Victorian box used in St George's Square, London; f. A post-box carved into a pillar at Hoverton, Norfolk

Trollope the Treatymaker

The new rail network opened new avenues to Trollope. He could cover his assignments more quickly and write at the same time. Sometimes he would travel on a train with several sheaves of paper propped up on a wooden tablet, and, to spare his blushes, hide behind a newspaper while he was writing. Most of *Barchester Towers*, second of the Barchester Chronicles series, was written this way. 'I wished to be more than a clerk at the Post Office. To be known as somebody – to be Anthony Trollope if it be no more – is to me much', he said. *Barchester Towers* was to bring the Trollopes a small regular income for several years.

In 1858 Trollope and his family visited his elderly mother and brother, Thomas Adolphus, at their home in Florence. Frances was still making a living from writing, but becoming increasingly frail. During the stay, Thomas Adolphus gave Trollope the idea for a plot about the medical profession. *Doctor Thorne* became Trollope's best-selling novel.

Later that year he was sent to make a postal treaty with Egypt, transferring all mail-carriage from the traditional camel routes across the Sahara Desert to steam train. The visit gave him the opportunity to finish another novel, *The Three Clerks*, an amusing parody on post office life, and to start *The Bertrams*, featuring a Victorian family. 'I was moved by a determination to excel, if not in quality, at any rate in quantity', he said.

In the autumn of 1858 the Post Office asked Trollope to improve the posts in the run-down city of Glasgow, and it was while trudging up and down the murky staircases of the city's tenement flats, that Trollope devised many of *The Bertrams*' love scenes. However, at the end of the year, duty called again. Trollope was asked to set up a new postal network in the West Indies and sign postal treaties with Grenada and Cuba.

Trollope the Theorist

Trollope now wished to be nearer London and its publishers. He applied for a transfer and was appointed Eastern England surveyor, the Post Office's most senior surveying position. Trollope, who was still only thirty-nine, moved with his family to a grand mansion called Waltham Manor at Waltham Cross in Essex, only 12 miles from London.

Yet Trollope was still treated with caution by the administrators at St Martin's-le-Grand, including the secretary, Rowland Hill. He and Hill had a number of disagreements, which the novelist referred to as:

> feuds – such delicious feuds! I was always an anti-Hillite . . . believing him to be entirely unfit to manage men or to arrange labour. It was a pleasure for me to differ from him on all occasions – and looking back now, I think that in all such differences I was right. With him I never had any sympathy, nor he with me. In figures and facts he was most accurate, but I never came across anyone who so little understood the ways of men – unless it was his brother Frederic. To the two brothers, the servants of the Post Office – men numerous enough to have formed a large army in the old days – were so many machines who could be counted on for their exact work without deviation, as wheels may be counted on, which are kept going always at the same pace and always by the same power.

Trollope also disapproved of the new civil service examinations that Hill had ushered in, describing them as 'the damnable system of promotion by so-called merit'. In 1863 he wrote to Hill:

> The theory of promotion by merit – that theory by which promotion is to be given, not to the senior man who is fit, but to the man who is fittest, be he the senior or the junior – is thoroughly Utopian in its essence; but it has in it, I think, this of special evil, which is not inherent in most Utopian theories, that it is susceptible of experimental action, and that the wider the action grows the greater is the evil done . . . a system in which a certain number of lads will best answer a string of questions, for the answering of which they are prepared by tutors who have sprung up for the purpose since this fashion of election has been adopted.

Trollope also had strong views on the quality of post office reports:

> I have written, I should think, some thousands of reports – many of them necessarily very long; some of them dealing with subjects so absurd as to allow a touch of burlesque; some few in which a spark of indignation or a slight glow of pathos might find an entrance. I have taken infinite pains with these reports, habituating myself to write them in the form in which

they should be sent – without a copy. It is by writing thus that a man can throw on to his paper the exact feeling with which his mind is impressed at the moment. A rough copy, or what is called a draft, is written in order that it may be touched and altered and put upon stilts. The waste of time, moreover, in such an operation, is terrible. If a man knows his craft with his pen, he will have learned to write without the necessity of changing his words or the form of his sentences.

Hill, who was a disciplinarian, was upset by Trollope's satirical novel, *The Three Clerks*, about Charley Tudor, a Post Office clerk, who gained his post by the traditional methods of favour and patronage, while his father Alaric, head of the new civil service examiners board, fell into bad company, took bribes and was eventually sent to prison for corruption. It was an obvious dig at Hill and the supporters of entry examinations. Hill's patience finally snapped when Trollope gave a humorous and irreverent lecture on the reformed civil service and its new examination structure to some newly recruited post office clerks. Hill went to the postmaster-general, the Earl of Hardwicke, and asked for Trollope to be dismissed, but his request was refused.

Despite the occasional disagreement with head office, Trollope enjoyed his new posting. 'The Post Office at last grew upon me and forced itself into my affections.' His writing also flourished. After *The Bertrams*, he started *Castle Richmond*, which he sold to the publishers Chapman and Hall for £600. Soon afterwards he was paid £1,000 by William Thackeray, the novelist and editor of London's *Cornhill Magazine*, to write a three volume series for the magazine. Trollope was also regularly meeting and entertaining writers like Charles Dickens, Elizabeth Gaskell, George Eliot, Wilkie Collins and Thackeray and, with six hunters in his Waltham stable, was leading the life of an Essex squire with a £4,500 salary to match.

In 1861 he started another project, this time a literary one. He was given a nine-month sabbatical by the Post Office to write a history of the North–South conflict in the American War of Independence.

Putting it in Writing

Trollope continued to refine his writing regime, paying his elderly groom an extra £5 a year to wake him each morning with a cup of coffee. He would then sit at his desk and spend half-an-hour reading his previous day's work before settling down to write for two-and-a-half hours at a rate of 250 words – or a page – every 15 minutes, his silver pocket watch ticking like a metronome in front of him. He would stop writing at approximately 8.30, when he would have his breakfast and set off for work at the Post Office. His niece who was living with the family would then make a neat copy of the morning's work. With such a regime, Trollope was able to finish his famous Palliser novels, a series he always regarded as his best, and write for magazines including his own, *The Fortnightly*, which featured politics, literature, philosophy, science and art.

In 1864, when Rowland Hill retired as Post Office secretary, he was replaced by Trollope's brother-in-law, John Tilley. When Trollope applied for the post of deputy secretary, he was turned down, the post going to a young post office official named Frank Scudamore. Trollope was very upset, believing his poor grasp of accounts had affected the decision, and his work at the Post Office began to lose its lustre.

> I was attached to the department, had imbued myself with a thorough love of letters – I mean the letters which are carried by the post – and was anxious for their welfare as though they were all my own. In short, I wished to continue the connexion. I did not wish, moreover, that any younger officer should again pass over my head. I believed that I had been a valuable public servant, and I will own to a feeling existing at that time that I had not altogether been well treated.

Three years later, on 3 October 1867, Trollope retired. Though he was only fifty-two, he and Rose now had enough money to support themselves for the rest of their lives. Despite his literary success, he wrote:

> It is absolutely true that during all those years I had thought very much more about the Post Office than I had of my literary work, and had given to it a more unflagging attention.

Now writing became his first priority, and he enjoyed finishing *The Last Chronicle of Barset*, which, like many of Dickens's novels, appeared in monthly instalments in a magazine. However, the Post Office hadn't forgotten

Trollope's negotiating talents and, in 1868, asked him for one last favour – to sign a treaty with the United States to speed up the transatlantic packet service.

Later that year Trollope stood as Liberal candidate for Beverley, Essex, in the general election. His manifesto described him as an 'advanced conservative Liberal', however, he failed to win the seat, mainly due to the number of staunch local Conservatives and his political honesty. The *Beverley Recorder* said:

> The Liberals fought heroically and nobly, and although well aware that the expenditure of a few pounds would have secured for them a successful issue, they rigidly abstained from giving even a glass of water to any voter.

Trollope was not at all disappointed as he had only stood after his uncle had made a half-serious wager with him about being a politician. Now Trollope could go back to writing and his output continued to grow. A trio of his works, *Phineas Finn, He Knew He Was Right* and *The Vicar of Bullhampton* were serialized in the leading London magazines. In 1870 he wrote three further novels.

> I had always had a pen in my hand. Whether crossing the seas, or fighting with American officials, or tramping about the streets of Beverley, I could do a little, and generally more than a little.

The following year, Trollope and his wife spent eighteen months in Australia with their eldest son, Frederic, a Melbourne sheep-farmer. During the two month voyage, he wrote the novel *Lady Anna* and later a guide to the new Australian colonies. On their return, the Trollopes moved to 39 Montague Square, London, Trollope spending at least three days a week hunting in Essex. He finished his series of six Palliser novels and wrote several serious books. Then, while he was nearing the end of his *Autobiography* in 1876, he began to suffer serious bouts of asthma. To improve his health, the family Trollope moved to the bracing air of Sussex. Soon afterwards the writer made a long trip to Italy and a shorter one to his beloved Ireland where he wrote his last novel *The Landleaguers.*

On 3 November 1882, Trollope had a stroke from which he never recovered and died at a nursing home in Welbeck Street, London, on 6 December. He was sixty-seven. A small funeral attended by the poet Robert Browning and artist J.E. Millais was held at Kensal Green church, London, where William Thackeray's funeral had been held twenty years before. Trollope was buried just a few feet from Thackeray's grave.

In his own way, the novel-writing reformer made almost as big a contribution to the Post Office as Rowland Hill. He helped create Britain's first network of letter-carriers, introduced the post-box to Britain, and signed many overseas treaties, as well as writing sixty books, forty-seven of them novels.

7

A Century of Surprises

We lately had our eyes very uncomfortably dazzled by the sight of
Postmen in glaring red uniforms, more fitted for the Fire Brigade than for
a peaceful body of men.

Punch, 2 June 1855

Legend has it that the Post Office issued London postmen with uniforms to find out which of them were 'loitering and mis-spending their time in ale houses'. However, it is more likely that the GPO wanted to give the job more status and to create a network of men who looked as smart as army captains. Whatever the reason, it helped make the GPO part of the British establishment – its official *literae humaniores* (letter-carriers).

The first postal employees to wear uniforms were stage-coach guards in 1784. Their outfits were mainly red – typifying the Post Office's royal status – and consisted of a scarlet coat with blue lapels and gold braiding, blue cloth waistcoats with brass buttons and gold-banded cocked hats made of beaverskin. The echo of the post-horn and the arrival of the gold and black coach-and-four with its resplendently uniformed guard became one of the symbols of the eighteenth and early nineteenth centuries.

However, uniforms had their opponents. Some MPs believed they would make London postmen too official-looking and of too military a bearing when visiting people's homes, while senior post office management thought them an unnecessary expense. Anthony Todd, joint Post Office secretary, said in 1792,'This good is not equal to the expense the Revenue would incur by clothing such a number of persons.' But the overall government view was that uniforms would make postmen smarter and inspire greater trust among the public when handing over money. A uniformed postman was less likely to be a victim of robbery, they said. So what did the postmen themselves think? They were unimpressed, fearing eye-catching uniforms would attract rather than deter robbers.

Nonetheless the first uniforms were issued to London postmen in the autumn of 1793. Discarding their raggedy clothes, they became part of a military-style team in their cutaway-style scarlet coats and fine leather wallets, which they slung elegantly over their left shoulders. There was one flaw in the new ensemble, however. They had to wear their own trousers. The Post Office believed official ones would attract dirt and present a poor overall image to the public.

So for year after year, trouserless red uniforms were issued to London's growing band of letter-carriers and in 1834, to the couriers of Edinburgh and Dublin, and gradually all the other city and town couriers. And in 1837, when members of London's twopenny post were issued with blue uniforms – again with no trousers – the humorists started drawing cartoons of postmen wearing negligees and nothing else! *Punch* followed with an article written in the form of a plea to Queen Victoria from a group of postmen's wives:

> Your petitioners humbly appeal to your Majesty's feelings as a wife. What would be your Majesty's feelings to see Prince Albert in the fine laced coat of a General (or a late Twopenny), with shabby trousers and boots not fit for any painter to take him in?

Finally, in 1855, the Post Office took the less-than-subtle hint and issued London letter-carriers with black cocked hats – as worn by Parisian postmen – red frock coats, waterproof capes, and . . . a pair of smart grey trousers. The June 1855 edition of *The Illustrated Glasgow News* commented:

> So brilliant and complete does the tout ensemble appear, even from the crown of the new hat to the tip of the ample tail of the red coat, not forgetting the yellow band round the hat and the leather wallet round the shoulder, that we are astonished at the liberality of the Government in the matter and cannot help thinking that the coats, or the cloth at least, must have been cabbaged from the Crimea [Crimean War].

Punch took a different view:

> We cannot comprehend the taste which has pinned a large pair of scarlet skirts to the coat of the Postman, and caused us to mistake him for a sentinel off his post, by his resemblance to a Foot Guardsman in one of

the new regulation wrappers. Considering there is a Reward payable for the apprehension of a Deserter, we wonder that half the Postmen in London are not taken into custody every night on suspicion. . . . We can see no necessity whatever for the military aspect which is given to these men; and indeed in these war times it is enough to alarm half the old women in London, to have their portals thundered at every hour of the day by men of military aspect. . . . We recommend the immediate abolition of this very martial attire, which is likely to cause some delay in the delivery of letters, by elevating the Postman into a very formidable rival to the Policeman, in those little flirtations with our female servants, which have often kept a sentimental Constable grunting hoarse-nothings into our housemaid's ear, while some burglarious gentleman has been emptying our neighbour's plate-chest.

Nevertheless, despite its earlier scepticism, the Post Office was pleased to see that uniforms succeeded in improving the postman's standing with his customers and gave him a new sense of public duty. The government agreed. In 1859 all national postmen, mail-train guards, mail-cart drivers, porters and labourers were issued with a distinctive scarlet uniform, and the following year, the London postmen, considered to be the élite of Britain's letter-carriers, were given a scarlet winter coat, with a lighter version for summer, two pairs of regulation trousers, a hat, a waistcoat and a cape.

Their country cousins, however, remained trouserless which prompted Liverpool's postmaster to write to GPO headquarters:

So long as the men have to furnish themselves with trousers, they will wear articles so shabby as to be a discredit to the Service, on the ground that their small wage will not enable them to provide better. It would greatly help to elevate the character of the men, especially in the eyes of the public, if they were clothed in a proper uniform throughout.

But nothing happened until 1861 when the government changed the colour of uniforms back to blue – and issued all provincial postmen with trousers for the first time. The blue uniforms were equally impressive, with the letters GPO embroidered on either side of a red collar, and the tunics buttoned all the way down the front similar to the nineteenth-century British soldier.

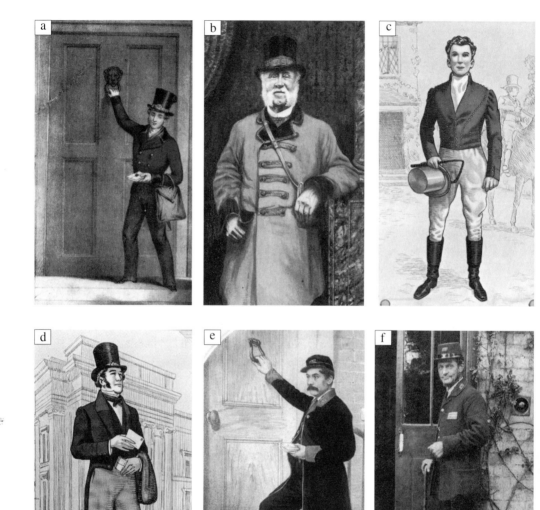

Postal uniforms were issued in 1793 after a long controversy about their 'military-style' appearance. Here is a selection from 1793 to 1880: a. The first London postman's uniform; b. Moses Nobbs, a popular mail-coach guard, in his scarlet tunic; c. A smartly-dressed post-boy; d. A district letter-carrier in 1837; e. A London postman in 1862; f. A photograph of Jonathan Wright, a Newport Pagnell postman, taken in 1880

The last employees to receive their own uniforms were telegraph messengers in 1870, which helped them look smart when delivering the magic telegram. Two years later the government added military-style stripes to all letter-carriers' uniforms, with three white stripes for 'regularity, diligence and fidelity' and four for 'superior activity, intelligence and devotion to duty'.

At the end of the nineteenth century carriers were referred to as 'Mr' when they arrived on people's doorsteps and many a maid would hide behind the door just before the day's first letter delivery and flirt shamelessly with Mr Postman while her master or mistress wasn't looking. After 1883, when parcels were introduced, all letter-carriers, whether working in the tiniest hamlet or London itself, were referred to as postmen. As a mark of their new status, they were issued with double-peaked shako hats – as worn by French postmen – which also helped keep the rain off their uniforms!

At the start of the twentieth-century, uniforms were designed more for comfort than spectacle. With a total of more than a hundred and ten thousand postal employees at their disposal, the government gave the Post Office a regular outfit of dark blue lounge-style jackets and trousers with red piping down the sides. The only exceptions were the London and Edinburgh postmen, who continued to wear Victorian tailcoats.

The only uniform that failed to impress anyone was issued in 1910, when postmen who rode bicycles were given billowing knickerbockers and puttees. Though the Post Office's aim was weather protection, all the outfits seem to have done was attract the curious glances and sniggers of passers-by, and in 1925 they were taken out of service. The knickerbockers would have been more suitable for the large contingent of women who joined the Post Office during the First World War. However, they were issued with their own pleasingly feminine blue serge skirts, capes and boots, with blue straw hats, which were later replaced by blue felt ones to go with the current fashion for bobbed hair.

After the First World War most GPO employees wore quiet-coloured versions of the two-piece suit. In 1932 the first peaked caps were issued to male postmen and in 1955, when annual summer temperatures began to rise, both men and women employees were given matching dark blue lightweight summer suits, with a heavier version for the winter.

Finally, in 1969, when it became a corporation, the Post Office adopted the colour grey for both male and female employees. This remained the standard colour for another fifteen years until 1984 when the GPO again reverted to its traditional dark blue suits with red-piped trousers.

Charismatic Cats

One day in the mid-1800s, the Post Office decided to issue contracts to cats. It was not for their charm as domestic pets or their ability to keep lonely postal clerks company. It was to help solve a serious problem – mice. For the little vermin were chewing letters containing banknotes and postal orders, especially at the Money Order Office (MOO). It had all become too much, and in 1868 the MOO controller asked John Tilley, the Post Office secretary, for a 2*s* a week allowance to pay for three energetic cats.

Tilley wrote back:

> Three cats may be allowed on probation – they must undergo a test examination and should, I think, be females. It is important that the cats be not overfed and I cannot allow more than one shilling a week for their support – they must depend on the mice for the remainder of their 'emoluments', and if the mice be not reduced in number in six months a further portion of the allowance must be stopped.

A month later the MOO controller wrote back to Tilley that after giving three cats a trial run they had proved highly successful. He would make sure they honoured their contracts. After a further six months the controller was able to write that the cats had performed 'exceedingly well', one of them had been catching twelve mice a night, and as a trio they had almost rid the office of mice. The cats had also honoured their contracts by not going to the extra expense of having kittens.

The controller then asked Tilley to give the cats a pay rise to cover their thirsty work – as one of the porter's wives had been spending 8*d* of her own money each week to pay for extra milk. Tilley duly obliged.

But mice were not the only problem. In 1873 the Post Office secretary was asked by Southampton sorting-office for a 1*s* 9*d* a week allowance to pay for a cat 'expert in the art of rat-catching'. Tilley replied that the salary they were asking was too high, after all a rat-catching cat could supplement his diet by eating his dead victims. But the determined Southampton management pointed out that a rat-eating cat would die as the rats lived on mail-bags and were vermin-infested. However, they eventually settled for a compromise salary of 1s a week to pay for a new troubleshooter. Several other offices followed suit. Accomplished rat-catchers joined the staff at Nottingham and Deptford sorting-offices, as well as at St Martin's-le-Grand itself, to help protect Her Majesty's Mail.

One of the rats' favourite haunts was the Post Office's London storehouse, where food and cooking utensils were kept, often in open packages. The storehouse manager wrote, 'Short of employing Peter Pan to spirit them away, I don't know how we are going to solve this problem.'

The Post Office duly obliged and sent them two large cats on six month contracts. Soon Post Office mice began to rear their greedy little heads again. A report from the Accountant-General's Department at Telephone House, London, in 1919, said, 'Telegrams have been eaten away by mice to such an extent as to be useless. Some of the ladies are rather perturbed. . . . ' It was a plea the gallant Post Office management could not refuse, and they gave the department a large mouse-catcher with an extended contract.

But perhaps the saddest event in postal cat history occurred in 1950 when, after twelve years' service at the 'Grand', the GPO's most famous cat, Minnie, died of tuberculosis. The Post Office held a special memorial service, attended by twenty senior officials. Faced with the problem of finding a successor the mourners put advertisements in *The Times* and the *Daily Telegraph*, which attracted twenty-five hopefuls, and for six days, personal interviews were held with the cats and their proud owners, until a suitable 10 lb replacement was found.

The subject of contracts for cats even reached the government's busy agenda when in 1953, during Parliamentary Question Time, assistant postmaster-general Sir David Gammans was asked by Captain L.P.S. Orr, MP, when 'the allowance payable for the maintenance of cats' was last debated. Gammans replied:

There is, I am afraid, a certain amount of industrial chaos in the Post Office cat world. Allowances vary in different places, possibly according to the efficiency of the animal and other factors. It has proved impossible to organize any scheme for payment by results or output bonus. . . . Except for cats at Post Office Headquarters, who got the special allowance a few years ago, presumably for prestige reasons, there has been a general wage freeze since July 1918. . . .

Captain Orr then asked if Post Office cats were given a family allowance, to which the assistant postmaster-general replied, 'The head-postmasters have full discretion to give a maternity grant which at the moment is very adequate.' And when a woman MP asked if Post Office tabbies and bitches received equal pay, Gammans replied, 'Equal pay has been accepted both in principle and practice in the employment of Post Office cats.'

At present there are more than four hundred postal cats in Britain and many sorting-offices regard them not only as essential rat and mouse deterrents but also affectionate colleagues. Sometimes a cat's career can span many years as it weaves in and out of the machinery and falls asleep on the postman's sack. Probably the longest-serving cat in recent times was Tibs, the giant 23 lb mouser, who died in 1964 after fourteen years' duty at Post Office headquarters. One of Tibs' successors, Blackie, who was paid £2 a week from 1971 to 1984, was renowned for her loud purring and appeared on the BBC's Nationwide programme and in a book about famous cats. Now that they have become an accepted part of post office life, cats no longer need contracts – just sharp claws.

Mouse Proud. Tibs the Post Office Cat, who successfully kept St Martin's-le-Grand vermin-free for fourteen years, weighed 23 lb when she died in 1964

Malicious Valentines

The Valentine card – that symbol of anonymous love – has not always had such a romantic aura.

In the early 1800s groups of pranksters sent malicious valentines which, instead of loving messages, bore unkind and cruel ones. And the unfortunate female victims had to pay the postman for these indignities when the cards were delivered. As a result the Post Office received a deluge of unhappy valentines, demanding their money back. The GPO, however, took a sympathetic view and usually repaid half or all the cost of postage. Eventually, the police caught most of the pranksters and fined them for their cruelty. And soon the unromantic habit died out.

In the 1830s valentines became all the rage. Each year more than sixty thousand were sent and postmen and sorters had to work overtime to cope with the extra workload. In some sorting-offices, sentimental postmasters would deliberately smudge the postmarks, so the recipients would not be able to recognize where the valentines came from.

It became a popular Victorian custom for a girl to peep through the keyhole before the postman arrived on Valentine's Day, and if she happened to catch sight of a cock and a hen together, it meant she was going to be married that year. Often romantically inclined young men would send valentines in the form of puzzle purses – several sheets of folded paper which, when unravelled, would reveal a ring. Sometimes the ring was wrapped in a pair of silk gloves, which the lucky valentine was supposed to wear the next time she went to church.

After the 1840 Penny Post, professional card-makers produced valentines with decorative drawings and verses by famous poets like Wordsworth, Keats and Shelley. One of the best known was Charles Whiting, who also helped design the early stamps, while the most famous was the De La Rue company, which later added envelopes and valentine playing-cards to their collection. However, the most unusual cards were a series of valentines that resembled five-pound notes, which were so realistic that they had to be withdrawn for security reasons.

The valentine fad largely died out during the 1850s but became popular again in the 1920s, known as the Roaring Twenties, when the wild, carefree spirit of the Charleston and foxtrot inspired Britain's young lovers once more.

Romantic Duo. Two housemaids and a dog greet Mr Postman on St Valentine's morning. From an 1876 painting

One of the favourites was a valentine telegram with drawings by the famous artist Rex Whistler.

Today valentines appear in many guises, loving, sentimental, rude, humorous and passionate. But their message of anonymous love is no different from the first valentine sent by royal courier from Miss Margery Brews to Mr John Paston of Norfolk, in 1477. Unfortunately his reaction was never recorded but the card is still on display in the British Museum.

8
The Quiet Revolution

Victorian post offices were like gossip parlours, where Mrs Johnson could tell Mrs Hawkins about the affair between the local gamekeeper and the vicar's daughter. They consisted of a room or two rooms in the postmaster's house with a table or counter at one end for postal transactions and a number of easy chairs at the other.

Before post offices, people had been picking up and delivering their post at receiving-houses.

> The public required little attention, and got but little. Being prior to the time of postage stamps, and we may also add of money orders, not to speak of savings bank business, few applications were ever made to the officers – consisting of the postmaster, his wife and a clerk – for anything but scraps of information relative to the despatch of mail. The communication with the public was anything but close, being conducted . . . through a trap-door in a wooden-pane in the office window,

wrote W. Lewins in *Her Majesty's Mails* in 1864.

One of the first post offices was opened in 1831 in the Scottish village of Crathie, near Balmoral. It looked like any other local cottage, with thick granite walls and a pitched roof. However, instead of family furniture and pot-pourri, the front room contained several fine oak chairs with a large oak dresser in the middle, where postal records were kept. Queen Victoria often walked across the fields from Balmoral Castle to chat to Crathie's postmaster Charles Thomson before buying stamps and posting her letters. When Thomson died, and his son, Albert, became postmaster, the queen personally paid his salary and for a new extension to the post office. Crathie post office was the first of many. After the Penny Post, offices, many of them fitted with

First Post. Letter volumes were still comparatively low in 1820 when Newcastle-upon-Tyne had
only one resident letter-carrier (above)

wooden counters for postal transactions, opened in all the major towns and cities.

Pillars of the Community

Post-boxes, too, began to sprout like mushrooms in the main settlements, making it easier for the man in the street to post his mail and the couriers to collect it. The first ones were painted green and treated as objects of mirth rather than worth. However, when they changed to red, people took them more seriously and they soon became welcome splashes of colour at drab street corners. The first London boxes were 5 ft high rectangles with an orb at the top. After that they appeared in many guises: tall, squat, hexagonal, square, octagonal and finally cylindrical like today's, and they all bore the initials VR, Victoria Regina.

In rural areas, wall-boxes were carved into the walls of country estates that overlooked village high streets. The first ones, made by a company called W.T. Allen, were installed at Shrewsbury and Market Drayton in 1857. One of their unique features was meant to be a cast-iron plate hanging over the letter

Royal Mail. Queen Victoria often bought stamps and posted letters at Crathie post office near Balmoral Castle in Scotland

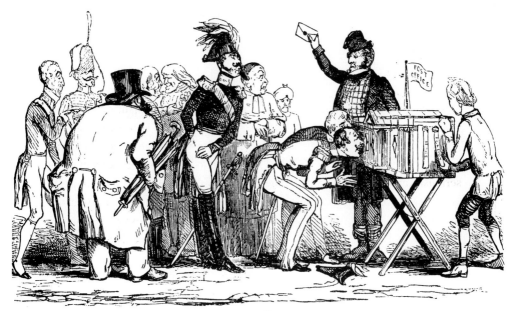

THE POST-OFFICE PEEP-SHOW.—"A Penny a Peep—Only a Penny!"

Viewing Time. *Punch* gives a comical version of Sir James Graham's letter-opening incident in 1844

slot. However, when it rained water would pour in and soak the mail. So the plates were replaced with weather-proof hoods. Recently a group of Oxfordshire villages was asked by the county council to replace their wall-boxes with modern post-boxes. But, upset with having to pay for the price of progress, the villagers put up the new boxes and then walled them in again.

The Sanctity of Letters

As the volumes of letters rose, postal security became a matter of public interest. Not only was the man in the street anxious that his letters did not go astray, newspapers too were concerned about the security of important national documents. Were 'top secret' letters from foreign embassies being opened by the government? Were letters sent by important people opened for political gain? asked the newspapers and public orators. The answer came in 1844 when *The Times* revealed that, on the orders of Home Secretary Sir James Graham,

Wall Unit. A post-box cut into a stone pillar at Martindale, near Ullswater, in the Lake District. Note the leak-proof hood

government officials had opened several letters sent from London to Italy by the exiled Italian leader Giuseppe Mazzini.

Graham told the House of Commons that he believed Mazzini was involved in an Italian plot to invade Europe. However, it emerged that his suspicions were groundless and his action was condemned by both the Whig opposition and members of his own party, who pointed out that the 1711 Letter Opening Act said the government could open letters only in 'very exceptional circumstances'. It even drew comment from the writer Thomas Carlyle who said,'This opening of men's letters is a practice near of kin to picking men's pockets.'

Graham publicly apologized to Mazzini, and a special inquiry revealed that the government had been using a secret letter-opening office since the previous century. In future, letters could only be opened with a special warrant from the secretary of state.

The Postman's Knack

Not only did the Penny Post lead to a nationwide letter-writing boom, it also speeded up the introduction of new post offices and post-boxes, while prepaid postage made the progress of a letter from A to B a simple operation. Envelopes protected letters from damage and displayed addresses more clearly, and, instead of having to buy one at a time, stamps were now sold in perforated sheets.

Soon another simple little device was added to the post's growing repertoire. In 1865 a German inventor, Dr Heinrich von Stephan, approached his national post office with an idea for a card that could carry short messages and did not need an envelope. But the Germans were unenthusiastic, pointing out that because of its small size the card would get lost in the system. Dr von Stephan then took his idea to the Austrian post office, who were immediately impressed and decided to adopt it. When Dr von Stephan brought the card to Britain in 1870, it again had a favourable reception and was introduced the same year with a halfpenny tariff. By the end of 1871, a total of one-and-a-half million postcards were being sent weekly in Britain.

However, another new postal item did not receive such a favourable reception. Thousands of magazines containing pornographic literature, many of them from the continent, flooded the system. This worried the government

Government Insider. A cartoon character called Paul Pry acts as a parliamentary letter-opener

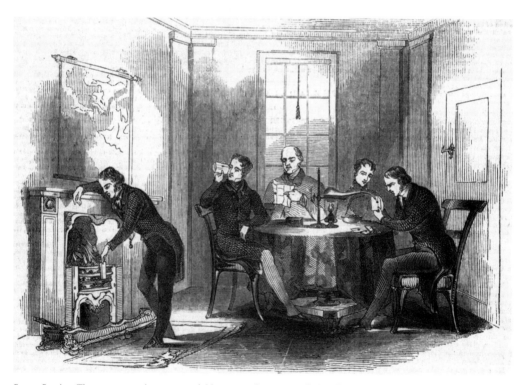

Secret Service. The government's controversial letter-opening room at St Martin's-le-Grand

who were anxious to keep public morals high and run a reputable postal service. A six year clean-up campaign by Post Office secretary John Tilley led to the 1870 Post Office Act which banned the sending of all 'indecent or obscene' literature.

During his sixteen years as secretary, Tilley and his assistant secretary Frank Scudamore led many such campaigns and managed to sustain Rowland Hill's quiet revolution. Tilley's first major reform was social, with the introduction of old-age pensions and life insurance at post offices in 1864. Next he turned to the newspaper rate. A total of two million were being sent out from London per week, and believing the penny an ounce rate was too high, Tilley lowered

Open Plan. The huge office at St Martin's-le-Grand that London postmen used for sorting in the 1840s before going out on their rounds

it to a halfpenny. Cheaper letter postage was his next priority. For the first time since 1840 he lowered the rate for 2 oz letters from 4*d* to 1½*d*, with ½*d* for every extra 2 oz. Finally, the telegram, which was introduced in 1837, had become too expensive. So, under the 1870 Telegraph Act, Tilley persuaded the government to take over all the private companies. The service was sub-contracted to the Post Office who subsequently reduced the telegram rates.

However, the takeover led to discord among the telegraphists who were lower paid than other postal employees, and in 1871, 219 telegraphists walked out. It was the Post Office's first official strike. At that time telegraphists had no union, so when management decided to suspend them, they went back to work without fuss. The Post Office later improved their working conditions.

The Streets with No Names

In the 1870s the average postman was aged twenty-two, 5 ft 6 in tall and weighed 9 st 6 lb. He earned 25*s* a week, and sometimes a little extra for making deliveries for private firms. However, some postmen had a reputation for drinking on duty and one who was suspended for alleged drunkenness was so upset that he wrote to Tilley: 'The slight smell of drink that the inspector noticed was what I and my missus had for our supper the night before.'

The ever-widening delivery network also had its problems. Most European countries had introduced house-numbering in the eighteenth century, and although it had started in Britain, there were still many houses with no numbers and streets with no names.

Couriers could be faced with addresses like:

> For dearie Mrs Hibbert
> The Cottage by the Wood
> Mr Thomas Hibbert's Farmer and all the rest of it
> If you take the Carriage Drive you'n find it to the right on you
> Mr Postman Titherington.

As a result, letters sometimes went astray, though local knowledge often came to the rescue of postmen who had worked in the same area for a long time.

Another tricky element was the Victorian floods. Perhaps the worst flooding

Personal Service. A village postman picks out a letter for an eager customer. From the *Illustrated London News* (1867)

occurred in 1874, when the water was up to 4 and 5 ft deep in some northern towns, and postmen had to stand on wooden carts and use long wooden poles to deliver letters through the top windows of houses. However, the floods also brought an unexpected bonus. The circulations of newspapers with stories of the chaos doubled and helped to boost postal revenues.

Spreading the Word

Several European countries had industrial revolutions similar to Britain's which led to expanding trade and bigger postal networks. Soon world mail volumes began to grow too. However many national posts were haphazard, with poorly marked boundaries, differing postal rates, and inconsistent methods of delivery.

It was time for someone to take the initiative. In 1862 Montgomery Blair, the American postmaster-general, wrote to fifteen post offices proposing a conference to solve the 'many embarrassments to foreign correspondence'. He had an outstanding response. The following year, fifteen national delegates, including Britain's Frederic Hill, met in Paris to discuss proposals for an international postal union. After the conference, hundreds of letters and petitions were sent to Blair about the scheme and it was also highlighted in the major international newspapers.

Years of discussion and debate followed until 1874 when twenty-two nations including the USA, Egypt and most of Europe met at Berne in Switzerland, and agreed to set up the Universal Postal Union (UPU) in 1875. The giant union, which agreed to meet every five years, immediately created a single territory for its members, thus helping to solve outstanding boundary and transport problems. It also introduced a standard 2½d rate for all letters under half an ounce. At its second meeting in 1880, the UPU set up an international parcel service with low standard rates of postage for members.

The same year, Henry Fawcett, a blind professor of political economy at Cambridge University, was appointed postmaster-general. Despite his disability, Fawcett was an energetic reformer, his first initiative being to negotiate with the railways for a cheap parcel service. Though the rail companies demanded 55 per cent of the revenue, a Parcel Post was introduced in 1883.

Fawcett's next move was to install special scales and cork hand-stamps at

Heavy Duty. A *Punch* cartoon showing the public's view of the 1883 Parcel Post and its creator, the blind postmaster-general Henry Fawcett

post offices to speed up the service. He also brought in the postal order to replace the traditional money order. The postal order was so popular that by the end of the nineteenth century, members of the public were sending almost two million a week. But they were easy victims of robbers and forgers, and it was an alleged case of postal order theft that turned into one of the unique court cases of the time.

It began when thirteen-year-old naval cadet George Archer-Shee went to his local post office in Osborne, Isle of Wight, and was seen cashing a postal order for 5*s*. However, it was made out to another cadet and the incident was reported to his college by the Osborne postmistress. As a result, Archer-Shee was expelled.

Convinced of his innocence, the boy's step-brother Major Martin Archer-Shee MP decided to fight the Admiralty's decision through the courts. After attracting much public sympathy, Archer-Shee's case was eventually heard in the High Court. However, the court found in favour of the Admiralty on a point of law. Undeterred, Major Archer-Shee got a re-hearing in the Court of Appeal. The appeal lasted four days, at the end of which the judge dismissed the Admiralty's case on the grounds of insufficient evidence.

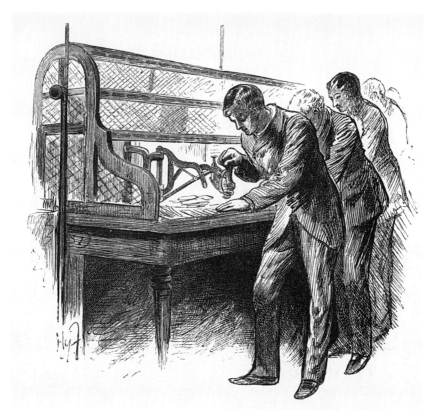

Marking Time. After 1883 senders used cork hand-stamps to mark the date and place on their letters

Major Archer-Shee was unhappy with the verdict, as he believed the young cadet should have been completely cleared of all blame. Thus, he and the boy's father used the press and parliament to attack the establishment for what they believed was an Admiralty whitewash. The case was later dramatized by Terence Rattigan in his play, *The Winslow Boy*.

The last major reform of the nineteenth century occurred in 1897 when the government passed a law stating that every house in Britain should have between two and three deliveries a week. By 1900 a total of one-and-a-half billion letters and sixty-seven million parcels were being sent each year. As postal historian Dr Alan Clinton said in *Post Office Workers*:

Branching Out. London's chief post office moved from St Martin's-le-Grand to a new building designed by Sir Henry Tanner, in nearby King Edward's Street in 1910. It now houses the National Postal Museum

The nineteenth century post office came to be seen as one of the great civilizing influences of Victorian England. It expanded from a small revenue-earning department of state to a big business with an enormous turnover.

It was the end of a quiet revolution.

9

The Merchants of Travel

'Can I please send this letter to Macau?'
'Certainly, and where does your cow live?'
Overheard in a post office at London's Barbican

The steam locomotive was the talk of the town – and village – as it rumbled through England's tranquil countryside. Its magic was not lost on the Post Office either as, one by one, locos started carrying a rising tide of mail. At first they helped relieve the workload of the stage-coaches by taking letters between major towns and cities. Then as new rail links were laid, the network widened, and by the end of the Victorian era, steam locos had become the Post Office's main carriers.

The first locomotive – or mechanical horse – to carry passengers and letters was George Stephenson's famous *Rocket*. In 1929 the *Rocket* and two other locomotives, the *Sans Pareil* and the *Novelty*, competed in a 'trial run' on a rough stretch of track at Rainhill, Liverpool. Watched by a large, cheering crowd, the locos hissed and puffed for several minutes before eventually chugging off down the 2 mile track. After half a mile the *Sans Pareil* began to slow down and then stopped altogether with a fuel problem, leaving the other two locos to battle it out. A few minutes later the *Novelty* started to splutter after she developed problems in her boiler and she too had to retire, leaving the *Rocket* to carry on and finish the contest. Stephenson's *Rocket*, which had travelled at an average speed of 29 mph, was thus acclaimed the winner amid scenes of much celebration. The following year she went into service as the world's first working locomotive, her unique design setting the standard for most of the early British locos.

The *Rocket* began operating on the Liverpool to Manchester line which opened in 1830. She was soon joined by several more locos as new tracks were laid next to the coach roads and the sight of the mechanical horses chugging by caused much merriment among stage-coach passengers. In 1838 a new contraption took to the rails. Shaped like a large horse-box, it was fitted to a

Rocket Post. The first steam locomotive, Stephenson's *Rocket,* started carrying letters on the Manchester to Liverpool railway in 1830

locomotive on the Birmingham to Warrington line, with a large batch of mail and several sorters on board. By the time the odd-looking horse-box had reached Warrington, all the mail had been franked and sorted. It was the railway debut of Rowland Hill's Travelling Post Office.

The TPO was an efficient and labour-saving way of carrying the post and became a regular fixture on the growing rail network, its bags of sorted mail being thrown into trackside chutes, later replaced by mail-catching nets, as the trains chugged through the stations. Not everyone approved of them, however. For they had poor ventilation and no seating or sanitation. On long journeys, postal employees could spend up to two days inside the TPO without a break which led a senior Post Office manager to remark, 'Few can bear the wear and tear of the travelling post offices. They can cause nausea and affect the brain and can lead to paralysis, nervous debility and mental derangement.' During one seven year spell, twenty-eight TPO sorters were overcome by oil-lamp fumes or lack of oxygen.

By 1855 many of today's major rail routes had been opened, and during the next half-century there was only one serious mail-train accident. On

Moving Experience. Travelling post offices had no ventilation and often gave sorters health problems

Travelling Light. A drawing of the inside and outside of an empty TPO soon after it was devised by Rowland Hill in 1826

28 December 1879 the Edinburgh to Aberdeen train was crossing the newly opened Tay Bridge when a furious storm blew up, pounding the iron-girdered bridge until it began to creak and sway. As darkness fell, a 300 ft long centre section gave way and, unable to stop, the train and its seventy-eight passengers plunged into the River Tay estuary. All the passengers were drowned, but most of a large consignment of mail was salvaged the next day from a beach 4 miles down river.

Another type of locomotive, powered by air instead of steam, took to the tracks in 1863. Built by the Pneumatic Despatch Company, this particular loco was never seen by the majority of the British public as it travelled underground. The pneumatic railway, which ran through a tunnel 9 ft below the streets of London, carried mail in 8 cwt wrought-iron cars between London's northwest sorting office in Eversholt Street to Euston station, the cars being sucked from one end to the other by atmospheric pressure. 'Doing the tube' became a fashionable pastime in contemporary London, one brave lady surprising the Euston sorters when she rode the entire 8 miles on top of a rail-car 'without injury to petticoat or person'. However, the subterranean railway, based on an idea of Rowland Hill, proved to be unprofitable, and was closed after four years. In 1873 a second underground line was opened between St Martin's-le-Grand and Euston, but it proved no more economical than the first, and survived three years.

Overseas Post

Sending a letter by sea was a rare event in the sixteenth century. Occasionally, the king or queen would despatch a courier to Dover with a letter for a foreign monarch, which would then be carried by merchant vessel. As the letters became more frequent, an occasional mail service was established, its vessels adopting such names as the *Post Boy* and the *Post Horse*. In the seventeenth century the service became more serious, and two more ports, Harwich and Falmouth, were used for sea-going mail to the Netherlands, Spain and Portugal.

At the same time, purpose-built packet-boats were introduced for short, continental postal trips. The small wooden sailing-ships, so named after the packets of government letters they carried, were armed against defiant merchant vessels and fishing-boats that regarded all mail-carrying as their

Air Mail. The pneumatic railway made its debut in 1863 when this batch of letters was sucked by air through a 6 mile tube from Eversholt Street to Euston station

sovereign right. Ocean-going post, meanwhile, was carried by larger sailing-vessels.

Britain's colonies were the post's first big customers, East India Company ships taking the mail to India via the Cape of Good Hope and another group of merchant vessels risking the hazardous voyage to the West Indies. Occasionally ships carried transatlantic mail from Falmouth to Newfoundland in Canada and Florida in the USA, though a fully fledged packet service to the United States did not start until 1755.

The most important local packet service in the seventeenth century was the Anglo-Irish. A joint effort between the English and Irish postal services, the three-packet service started carrying post across the Irish Sea between

Holyhead and Dun Laoghaire. But, during the next hundred years, volumes became too much for the Irish Post Office to handle, and in 1784 they asked the GPO to take over the two-way service and give the Irish PO an annual retainer of £4,000. The English agreed and immediately introduced new packets to cope with the flourishing service. However, after a few years, the Irish Post Office began to resent the low retainer they were receiving and introduced their own packets called wherries, which were smaller and slower than the English ones. Soon there were mid-sea skirmishes between the two fleets, with the wherries usually coming off worst. The little packets were also unable to handle the large mail volumes between the two islands and delays crept into the service. The Irish Post Office withdrew them later, the English Post Office doubled their annual retainer to £8,000, and normal service was resumed.

During the eighteenth century the transatlantic postal service came into its own. Bigger and stronger packets successfully negotiated the tempestuous Atlantic ocean until the start of the American War of Independence in 1775 when during eight years of conflict, forty-three packets were sunk and nineteen badly damaged in mid-ocean skirmishes with American privateers. Nonetheless the service survived, though it still had to cope with natural hazards like icebergs and rats, which moved the postmaster-general to report to a packet captain after one trip, 'We are concerned to find the letters brought by your boat to be so consumed by rats that we cannot find out to whom they belong'.

The next sea-going hazard was man-made. One day a pair of customs officers boarded two packet-boats at Falmouth to find they were carrying illegal cargoes of tea and tobacco. On being accused of smuggling, the two packet captains and their crews mutinied, as they believed they were being victimized. The rest of the port then went on strike, trying to blackmail their employers by demanding higher wages in return for going back to work. When the management refused, the protesting workers marched on the Falmouth packet office. But the harbour chiefs called their bluff by moving the packet service to Plymouth, and the workers were left without a harbour and a job. Three months later the management relented, reintroducing the service to Falmouth, and the workers were given back their jobs.

Smuggling was a worrying trend in Britain's southern ports and even created its own form of élitism. On one particular packet trip from Falmouth to

Portugal, a Lisbon port official was amazed to see the ship divide the profits from its spoils strictly in order of seniority, the English captain receiving £5,000, the officers £2,500 each, and the able seamen £1,000 – a sort of honour among sea thieves.

Eventually dockside security was tightened and packet smuggling became sea lore. Petty theft was the next scourge, especially on large private mail-carrying ships and in 1799, the GPO opened a Ship Letter Office to supervise all private letter-handling. Captains were paid twopence for each sea-going mail item, the payment making them legally bound to carry it to its destination. Failure to do so meant imprisonment.

The Napoleonic Wars

The most spectacular tales of the sea-going post occurred during the Napoleonic Wars of 1803–15. In 1803 the *Lady Hobart* packet was making her return voyage from Nova Scotia across the Atlantic when she was attacked by a French privateer. After a two-hour battle, the packet successfully repulsed the enemy vessel and was continuing the crossing when fate struck again in the form of a giant iceberg that appeared out of the mist. Unable to steer clear, the *Lady Hobart* was hit amidships, all the mail and most of her crew disappearing into the sea. Another Napoleonic skirmish had a captive audience.

One hot, sunny afternoon, the *Duke of Marlborough* packet was attacked by a privateer in full view of Falmouth harbour. Crowds lined the headlands as the two boats clashed, their sails billowing and their cannons flashing and sputtering. For several hours they chased each other to and fro across the harbour, and twice the French tried to board the English vessel, only to be driven back by the English crew's swords. Finally, with six wounded and one dead, the *Duke of Marlborough* frightened off her French adversary. As a post-battle tribute, John Bull, the ship's captain, wrote: 'All stood to their quarters like lions; I scarcely know an instance in which the character of the British seaman has been more nobly and gallantly sustained'. The crew were rewarded with an extra four months' pay.

Gallantry also saved a Barbados-bound cargo of mail. The *Windsor Castle* packet was nearing the West Indian islands when she was attacked by a French privateer. During a three hour duel she managed to draw alongside the enemy vessel while five crew members, led by acting captain, William Rogers,

Sea Skirmish. A Post Office packet-ship battles with a French privateer during the Napoleonic Wars

boarded the vessel, and despite being outnumbered by ninety men, succeeded in capturing it. The plucky packet was thus able to complete its Barbados delivery. To mark his heroism, Rogers was given the Freedom of the City of London.

The Age of Steam

The discovery of steam revived the battered ocean postal service. The first 230 ton steam-packet was launched at Dover in 1818 and showed an eager Post Office what its embattled sailing-ships had been missing – strength, speed and capacity. After introducing steam-packets into the continental service, the Post Office decided to give two large steamships a trial with a Great Sea Race between the 1,340 ton *Great Western*, designed by Brunel, and the 700 ton *Sirius*, currently in service on the Irish Sea. On 4 April 1838 the *Sirius* set off from Cork with a large cargo of mail. Four days later the *Great Western* left Bristol with several hundred passengers, 600 tons of coal and a consignment of mail. Fifteen days later the *Great Western* steamed into New York harbour just a few hours after the *Sirius*, to great acclaim from a crowd of American enthusiasts. The *Great Western* was the new flagship of the transatlantic service.

Steamships became the rage. In 1840 the new Cunard line started a fortnightly mail service from Liverpool to Halifax, Boston and Quebec. Then a P&O service was launched from Southampton to Asia and the Far East, plus a new series of steam-packet routes to the British colonies, the most challenging of which was India as, half-way through the voyage, the bags of letters had to be carried across the Sahara Desert by relays of camels and donkeys.

Like the mainland Travelling Post Offices, steam packets and ships had their own on-sea sorting in large cabins called Sea Post Offices. One of the first SPOs was fitted to a newly built 46,000 ton ship, the *Titanic*. It went into service in April 1912, when the *Titanic* – or the 'unsinkable' – set off on her maiden voyage from Southampton to New York. On board were 1,513 passengers and 3,500 mail-bags guarded by five sorters. The crossing was smooth and incident-free, the passengers sometimes coming out on to the deck to enjoy the ocean sunshine. The *Titanic* was approaching the North American coast near the Grand Banks of Newfoundland, when a 'huge black mountain loomed out of the night', striking the ship's bows. The nervous passengers clambered to the deck to see a massive iceberg carving into the great ship's hull. Shouting and screaming, they fought to uncouple the lifeboats as water cascaded into the gaping hole. Then, with an almighty roar, the *Titanic* went down, taking many of the passengers and crew with her. Though 700 were later rescued, thanks to some skilled radio telegraphy by the ship's crew, all the mail was lost, a newspaper obituary recording how the sorters 'completely disregarded their own safety when the vessel sank, and began to carry the 200 sacks of registered mail to the upper deck'. The fate of the unsinkable *Titanic* is now a well-known sea story.

Inland Post

The speedier steam locomotive proved a natural successor to the stage-coach. TPO-equipped trains ran on all routes until 1885 when streamlined night expresses with horse-drawn coaches linked the main inter-city routes, the last surviving mail-coach clanking into London with the Newmarket mail on 15 January 1864. In the 1880s postmen rode centre-cycles, with a large front wheel, and four small ones at the back – which gave rise to the name, the hen-and-chickens – though postmen were forbidden from travelling more than

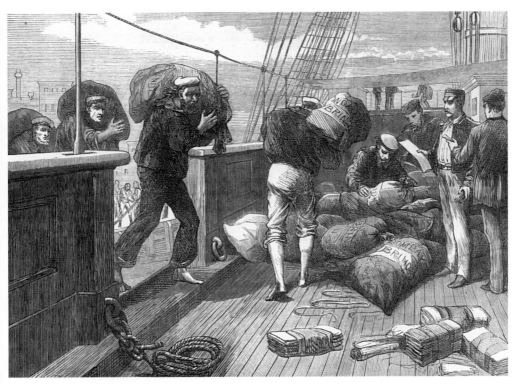

Moveable Feast. The home-bound mail is loaded on to a British steam packet-ship at the port of Brindisi, Italy, in 1872 (from the *Illustrated London News*)

28 miles per round, for fear of exhaustion! The hen-and-chickens was succeeded by the more practical penny-farthing, which had a single small rear wheel, or farthing. Meanwhile, postmen who needed to carry heavier items were issued with dog-carts.

In 1900 petrol-driven Daimlers began delivering the mail and attracting many admiring glances at the same time. The first motor roads were opened from London to Redhill and Manchester to Liverpool and by 1910, the Post Office had seventy motorized mail routes at its disposal. It launched the new service with a fleet of ninety-eight pillar-box red vans for long trips and some classic Model T Fords for shorter ones. Motor cycles and motor cycle combinations were also used to carry heavy mail items within towns and cities.

Perhaps the most radical transport idea occurred in 1927, when an electric underground rail system was launched in London. Remote-controlled trains

Easy Rider. Postmen who delivered the mail on penny farthings were not allowed to travel more than 28 miles per round – for fear of exhaustion

linked the capital's main sorting-offices with Liverpool Street and Paddington stations along a 6½ mile track, the electric underground speeding up the outgoing mail as it wound its way at 35 mph under London's interminable traffic queues. Further links were added until the subterranean post was carrying mail to eight main-line stations at the rate of sixty thousand mail-bags a day.

Letters take Flight

Messing about in hot-air balloons became a craze in the Victorian era. The phrase 'getting a bit of country air' had a new meaning as these voluminous creatures and their crews floated gracefully over towns, villages and parks. Thoughtful balloon owners sometimes helped out their local sorting-offices by delivering mail for them. However, despite their owners' good intentions, balloons did not prove to be a very reliable form of transport, especially when enthusiastic 'balloonatics' had to be rescued from the sea after their crafts had been blown off course.

The first reliable airmail flight occurred on 9 September 1911, when German aviator Gustav Hamel piloted a Bleriot monoplane from Hendon airport to Windsor Castle with a batch of letters to mark the accession of George V (see Chapter 15). However, when the plane's return trip was delayed by a storm, the Post Office became sceptical about airmail transport, stating in a report: 'An aeroplane is at present so dependent on the weather that it is practically useless as a means of ordinary and regular transport'.

It was not until 1919 that the mail really took flight. On 14 June aviator John Alcock and navigator Lieutenant Arthur Whitten-Brown attempted the first transatlantic flight when they took off in their Vickers-Vimy aeroplane from St John's, Newfoundland, with a cargo of 196 letters and a large parcel. The world held its breath as occasional sightings of the plane were reported by passing steamers. Then, sixteen hours later, the plane was seen approaching Ireland's west coast. Within a few minutes the two aviators landed at Clifden airport with all the letters, the parcel and themselves intact.

The Post Office changed its mind about air travel, and commissioned a fleet of RAF planes to deliver mail between London and Paris. Calling the new service 'super-post', the GPO eventually signed an agreement with the French post office in September 1919. It was the world's first airmail post. The first air letters cost an expensive 2s 6d each, until two years later the government reduced the rate to 2d an ounce.

Tunnel Vision. An underground railway linking London's main sorting-offices and stations was opened in 1927. The early trains (above) were little different from today's (below)

Britain's first main carrier was Imperial Airways, which chartered flights to Cairo, Baghdad, Bombay and Sydney. Imperial also experimented with different types of aircraft, one of which, a De Havilland DH50, took off from Australia with floats under its wings and landed several days later in the lower reaches of the River Thames. The flying-boat was to become a regular postal carrier with its long range and 3 ton capacity. Soon the aeroplane became the Post Office's main international courier, replacing the romantic steamship.

It was not long before Britain's inland mail took to the air as well, with a service between the Orkney Islands and Inverness in Scotland. The Post Office then started an air post linking London's Heathrow airport, with Liverpool's Speke and Derby's East Midlands airports, which expanded into an inter-city service called Skynet, helping to relieve road and rail congestion between Britain's major towns and cities. The Post Office's Skynet service now carries three-and-a-half million items a day.

The Space Invaders

At one stage it looked as if airmail might give way to space mail. In 1934 a German philatelist called Gerland Zucker surprised residents of the Sussex village of Rottingdean when he wheeled a U7 rocket on to the village green. With a hiss and a roar the rocket soared into space, landing in a field 5 miles away with 2,864 letters on board. But this was merely a trial run. Zucker was determined to start a regular space service between Scotland and the Outer Hebrides, and in July 1934 built a rocket site on the Hebridean island of Scarp. A large crowd of spectators gathered as a 130 ft rocket was lowered on to the launching pad, its fuselage daubed with the slogan 'Western Isles Rocket Service'. There was a hush as the gleaming object sputtered into life, flames spurting from its base. Then, as it roared into the sky, the rocket exploded in a great ball of flame. Fortunately not one of the three hundred spectators was hurt, though a batch of 130 slightly charred letters had to be carried by more orthodox methods to its destination on the Island of Harris. When Zucker subsequently applied to the Home Office for a rocket licence, it was refused.

One space delivery that did succeed, however, occurred in 1967 when American astronauts Neil Armstrong, Michael Collins and Edwin Aldrin made the first landing on the moon in the Apollo XI satellite. To mark the event, Neil Armstrong posted a letter marked 'Moon Landing' on the moon's surface.

High Flyer. Philatelist Gerland Zucker
(left) launches a letter-carrying rocket on
Lymington golf-course, Hampshire (below).
However, the craft came to a sticky end
when it landed in a nearby marsh

Broken Dreams. Zucker (inset) examines the wreckage after his rocket post exploded on take-off
at Scarp Island in the Outer Hebrides

10
London Calling

There was another ring at the front door. Jeeves shimmered out and came
back with a telegram.

Jeeves Takes Charge, by P.G. Wodehouse (1881–1975)

The telegram bewitched the Victorians with its charms. It was neat and easy to
read and could pass on news of births, marriages and deaths almost instantly.
However, its origins were both strange and scientific. It all began in 1816 when a
man named Francis Ronalds coiled an 8 mile long wire, with a dial at each end,
round and round his garden in Hammersmith, London. With the coil in place,
Ronalds switched on an electric current, and watched as one of the dials began to
form a letter in a square. It was the world's first attempt at sending a telegraph.
The idea was then developed by what could be described as a scientists' action
group. The physicist Charles Wheatstone, inventor of the harmonica, and
William Cooke adopted Ronalds' technique and sent the first message by electric
cable, which they then patented. Next Samuel Morse, of morse code fame,
Thomas 'the light bulb' Edison, Lord Kelvin, founder of the transatlantic
telegraph, Charles Bright, and Guglielmo Marconi carried out a series of
experiments and tests which led to the first commercial telegraph. Punched in
code on a reel of tape, it travelled via cable to a receiving operator who then
deciphered the code. When written down, the telegraph code became a telegram.

The first operator was a private company at Chalk Farm, London, which
started sending telegraphs in 1837. Then two railway companies set up a line
linking the stationmasters of Euston and Camden Town. Britain's first public
line was opened between West Drayton and Paddington railway stations in
1842, and it was not long before its powers were put to the test. One morning
the stationmaster of Slough, near West Drayton, noticed a suspicious-looking
character climbing into a passing train. He went into his little telegraph office
and punched out a message to Paddington, and two hours later when the train
arrived at Paddington, a couple of policemen were waiting to interview the
dubious traveller. It was a fair cop, for he was wanted for murder.

Nearly all the early telegraphs were used as station intercoms for train arrivals and departures. It was only later that they were used for telegrams. Each railway telegraph office had a dial in a glass case with two needles that clicked together whenever there was an incoming message. Often the sleepy clerks brought their dogs to work, so that they could fall asleep between cables. Then, when the needles clicked, the dogs started barking and woke them up.

Soon private telegraph firms started sending telegrams for members of the public. But it was a costly service. The price of a twenty word message was 1s, with 2s for forty words, while a twenty word telegram to Ireland cost 6s. It did not put the public off, however. A telegram was an ideal way of passing on news of a big occasion, be it a betrothal, a celebration or a crisis. The first one ever sent was to report a crisis. In it, Mrs Lovell of Wimborne, Dorset, warned Mr Shaw of Wednesbury, Staffordshire: 'James is dangerously ill. If Jane wishes to see him, she had better come immediately.'

The telegram also attracted a large overseas following. In 1865 Dr Heinrich von Stephan, the German inventor of the postcard, and several user-friendly countries set up the International Telegraph Union. The telegram's money-making potential began to appeal to the British government, and in 1870 the state bought out Britain's private telegraph companies and subcontracted the network to the Post Office. The GPO extended the number of lines, and by the end of 1871 ten million telegrams were being sent a year. It soon found a niche in British public life, sending news of major sporting events around the country and supplying news items to national and provincial newspapers. It also sent Greenwich Mean Time signals to station and office clocks. Now that telegram sending had become a public service, the government decided to play fair and reduce its price, and in 1885 a twelve word message could be sent for as little as 6d.

However, there was a flaw in the armoury. The thirteen- and fourteen-year-old messengers who delivered telegrams were paid only 5s a week, and as they grew older were sacked and replaced with younger, cheaper labour. In 1890 the newly formed Postal Telegraph Clerks Association pressed the government to improve their conditions. The response was immediate. Not only were the messengers' wages raised, but they were issued with smart new uniforms. The postmaster-general, H.C. Raikes, said:

It should be impressed on the boys that, wearing as they do the uniform of the Queen, they are under an obligation to conduct themselves in a manner which shall never bring that uniform into disrepute.

The messengers, who spent long hours of idleness between messages, were given special rest-rooms where they could cook meals and play cards, dominoes and parlour games. They also attended daily drill sessions in which they learnt to march and salute. The job had acquired a dignity all of its own.

The service reached its peak in 1900 when ninety million telegrams were sent. Then another invention, the telephone, began to take its place and by 1927 a mere forty-seven million telegrams were being sent a year. But the telegram still had a unique place in a crisis or an anniversary, and in 1935 the Post Office introduced goodwill telegrams for high-days, holidays, birthdays

Workers' Playtime. The telegraph messengers' rest-room where they played games and cooked meals between jobs

and anniversaries. And the knock on the door and the excitement of opening it to find a breathless messenger with a bright yellow envelope marked 'Telegram' was always a moment to treasure.

The last telegram was sent in 1982. The telephone, the telex and the fax had finally knocked it off its valuable perch.

Telephones

A fashionable Victorian saying described the telephone as 'an ideal instrument with which to call up one's Continental friends'. However, its origins were far more rudimentary.

After more than two years of trial and error, Scots engineer Alexander Graham Bell was experimenting with sound waves at his laboratory in Boston, Massachusetts, in 1876 when he heard a sound unlike any he had ever heard before. Coming out of one of the cables was the voice of his assistant, Thomas Watson, who was in the next room. The astonished Scotsman spoke back: 'Mr Watson, come here, I want you!' It was the voice of triumph, for Watson duly appeared at the doorway. Bell had invented the first telephone.

A few weeks later Bell put his new discovery to the test, linking his parent's home with a nearby house in Brantford, Ontario. He then sat some 8 miles away with a transmitter and receiver and, after a few minutes, was able to hear the distinct sounds of talking and music coming from the two houses. His ears had not deceived him after all on that extraordinary day in Boston.

In 1877 Bell staged a special demonstration for Queen Victoria at Osborne House in the Isle of Wight. She was so impressed that she asked the British government to adopt the idea. Bell put up several individual lines 'via a central office where the wires can be connected together as desired, establishing direct communications between any two places in the city of London'. It was the forerunner of the telephone exchange, the first of which was opened by the Telephone Company at 36 Coleman Street, London, in 1879.

Suddenly the competition for telephone lines started fizzing fiercely. Sometimes a company would put up a series of rooftop cables only to return another day to find they had been spiked by saboteurs from a rival company and replaced with a new set. On many occasions London pedestrians looked up to see rooftop skirmishes between opposing engineers. On other occasions cable companies would dig holes ready to install telephone poles, only to have them filled by the poles of a rival company. Disputes were frequent, and often had to be settled in the law courts.

Telephone design also attracted competition. The first black enamel telephones were large and cumbersome and weighed about 5 lb. But, wanting to project a streamlined, high-tech image, the telephone companies produced their own – and came up with a range of the most bizarre-looking specimens. The idea of actually using them for making contact seemed to be purely incidental.

Not surprisingly, many of the older generation were shy about using these odd talking-machines and only resorted to them in emergencies. Even the younger generation were intrigued that they could pick up a receiver and talk to someone several hundred miles away.

Soon general stores and chemists installed Silence Cabinets – or wooden kiosks – at the back of their shops for members of the public. It was usually only the shopkeeper's favourite customers or those who had paid their bills on time who were allowed to use them. The first public box – 2 ft taller than today's – went up in Bristol in 1886. It had automatic door-locks that could only be opened by inserting two halfpennies in a slot; others were manned by attendants who dialled the customer's call to the operator and collected the money afterwards.

Members of the upper-middle classes had two telephones installed in their homes; businessmen arranged to have the morning newspapers read to them by the office junior before going to work; owners of horses put telephones in their stables so that they could call up the groom when they wished to go riding; and some offices had gold-plated ones to impress visiting clients.

The government even bought some of the telephone lines, which they sub-contracted to the Post Office. The others were owned by the United Telephone Company, the National Telephone Company and the Lancashire and Cheshire Telephone Company, who paid the GPO a 10 per cent licence fee. When the three companies merged to form the National Telephone Company in 1889, they introduced a night telephone service for Members of Parliament.

The first telephone exchanges were manned by young boys, who got up to all sorts of mischief, playing pranks on callers, turning up late for work, and putting customers through to wrong numbers. So they were replaced by 'responsible' young women, many of whom had more than just pleasant voices. A National Telephone Company recruitment leaflet said applicants must be pretty, uncommonly quick-witted, with good general knowledge, insight into knowing what people mean to say when they cannot say what they mean, and have a pleasing, friendly and reassuring manner.

As a result, male callers were sometimes so attracted by the young women's pleasing, friendly and reassuring manners that they asked them out or even proposed to them. The young ladies' colleagues at directory enquiries had a harder time, however, and were nicknamed the 'conundrum girls' because of the tricky requests they had to handle.

In 1891 the telephone went international when a link was established between London and Paris. By the end of the nineteenth century, just over two hundred thousand telephones were being used in Britain to call up 'one's continental friends' as well as one's local ones.

The government finally bought out the National Telephone Company in 1912, and asked the hard-working Post Office to operate Britain's new public telephone service. Until then all telephone kiosks had been made of wood. Now the first cast-iron one went up in Holborn, London, shortly followed by a fully-automatic telephone exchange at Epsom, Surrey.

Two years later the telephone became a vital instrument of war. Not only was it an essential link between the government and the home and overseas forces, but thousands of telephone engineers were recruited to build radio and radar stations to detect enemy telephone transmitters and sight enemy aircraft and Zeppelins.

Now telephone kiosks were being built for strength rather than comfort. After the first cast-iron models, kiosks were made of concrete and exceedingly difficult to operate. So the designers went away to think again. In 1922 the architect Giles Gilbert Scott introduced a smaller version of the cast-iron box, with little windows in the sides. It was a winner. He later designed a more streamlined version with larger windows called the Jubilee Kiosk to mark King George V's silver jubilee in 1936.

Three years later the telephone helped Britain win the Second World War. Walkie-talkies, links between airports, gun- and searchlight-bases, and forces' telephone networks all helped the allied war effort. And the reassuring tones of 'London Calling' were to cheer up many a homesick overseas regiment. But perhaps the most impressive network was built during the 1944 D-Day landings when a system of telephone lines, switchboards and teleprinters was installed along the south coast for the British and French troops.

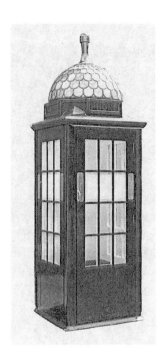

Twin Peaks. Just two of the many telephone kiosk designs submitted to the Post Office in 1924

The war certainly left its mark. Two million British telephone lines were destroyed as operators struggled to carry on in noisy, nerve-wracking conditions. One operator who survived a five hour ordeal was Mary White, who ran the Yorkshire village of Kirby Muxloe's telephone exchange from her cottage. During the Blitz, Kirby Muxloe was hit by two bombs during an air raid, the power of the blasts wrenching off the front door of Miss White's cottage, smashing windows and shutters, tossing furniture to and fro, snapping telephone wires, and finally showering Miss White in a hail of glass and falling plaster. Undeterred, she continued to receive incoming and outgoing calls until the attack subsided, her little Scottish terrier quivering in her lap. For her bravery, Miss White was awarded the King's Gallantry Medal.

Normal service was resumed in 1945 and by 1950 there were more than five million telephones in Britain. In 1958 STD (Subscriber Trunk Dialling) was introduced, which meant people could telephone any part of Britain without having to contact the operator. The first STD call was made by the Queen when she telephoned the Lord Provost of Edinburgh from a Bristol phone-box. The Post Office's next breakthrough was the opening of the 589 ft high Post Office Tower in 1966. It linked London to all Britain's telephone exchanges and could handle a hundred and fifty thousand simultaneous telephone conversations and transmit more than forty television channels. Later a 40 ft mast was added which could detect storms and was linked to the London Weather Centre. By 1981 almost two hundred thousand employees were working in the GPO's telephone department, compared with a hundred and eighty-nine thousand in the posts, so the government made it a separate public corporation. Three years later British Telecom went private.

Today telephones are more common than televisions. Hard as you might try, you cannot ignore them. They pop up on the underground, the beach, the golf-course, the pub and the supermarket and more than three million British-driven cars have built-in telephones. The telephone market has become as competitive as those early days of skirmishes on London's rooftops and telephone pole-swapping. British Telecom is still dominant in the home and office sector, though Mercury Communications has proved itself an impressive competitor, while in the mobile telephones sector, a flurry of companies are vying to prove that theirs are the cheapest and most user-friendly models.

Telexes

The telex is a high-tech telegraph that sends coded messages by teleprinter. Like the telegraph, it uses cables, radio and satellites to link up its subscribers. Until 1981 the service was run by the Post Office, now it is the responsibility of British Telecom.

The first telex – short for teletypewriter exchange service – trials were held in 1922, when engineers used typewriters instead of punching machines to send messages over telegraph lines. When the commercial network began ten years later, companies found they were able to send messages with the speed of the telephone and the authority of the written word. It also meant that any legally binding contracts they drew up could be signed in one day, instead of three or four.

In 1961 the first international telexes were sent from Britain to the then Federal Republic of Germany. The Post Office also opened a London Telex Bureau at Houndsditch, East London, and a series of exchanges that provided a twenty-four hour service for British companies. The network continued to expand, helping small companies to grow and prosper, medium-sized ones to expand into bigger, more effective ones, large businesses to become public limited companies and private corporations to become multinationals.

Today there are a hundred thousand British telex users. Some own their sending-and-receiving apparatus, while others hire them from British Telecom. However, the telex is unable to compete with another Post Office product, the fax.

The Fax

The fax, a faster and more direct method of message-sending than the telex, can reprint documents thousands of miles away in ten seconds. But it has taken a long time coming. For this quickfire product is a modern version of the chemical telegraph invented by Alexander Bain as far back as 1842 when for the first time an image – albeit blurred – of a written document or drawing could be sent by cable.

The first fax machines were used by the USA-based Associated Press to send facsimiles (or faxes) of photographs to newspapers in 1935. The fax's powers were then extended to weather maps, mechanical drawings, graphs, quotations, contracts and even fingerprints.

The British Post Office adopted the service and in 1948 produced the first Desk Faxes, enabling companies to send pictures of documents – or phototelegrams – to other companies via the telephone network. The phototelegrams improved and became faxes, able to reproduce a fair image in half-an-hour, and by 1968 it took about six minutes to send a printed page by fax.

In 1980 the Post Office opened the world's first international fax centre, Intelpost, in London, followed by a hundred and fifty nationwide and about two thousand five hundred worldwide. Today most fax machines are sold over the counter at ever-decreasing prices, with at least twenty companies trying to catch the consumers' eye. There are more than three million of them in British homes and companies, and the number is rising by the week, as people opt for the speediest method of 'putting it in writing'. Telecommunications have come a long way since that first electric wire coiled round a suburban garden.

11
In Times of Peace and Strife

If I could save the Union without freeing any slave, I would do it; and if I
could save it by freeing all the slaves, I would do it; and if I could save it
by freeing some and leaving others alone, I would also do that.
Letter from Abraham Lincoln, a former US postmaster, to a colleague in
1862

Inspired by the industrial revolution, Britain shrugged off its insular
nineteenth-century outlook and started selling itself to the rest of the world.
Industry saved and prospered. At the same time employee movements were
formed, for employers paid very low wages and workers were often sacked
without notice.

Such an event occurred in 1890 when, after staging a massive protest over
low pay, four hundred and fifty postmen were dismissed by the Post Office.
The next year the Postmen's Federation was formed, with Charles Churchfield
of London's East Central District Office as its general-secretary. However, it
was not the first postal union. In the previous decade, the Postal Telegraph
Clerks (1881) and the United Kingdom Postal Clerks (1887) associations
began, while the Fawcett Association of sorters – named after the blind
postmaster-general Henry Fawcett – was formed in 1890.

To most employers, unions were seen as unruly elements of disruption that
upset the smooth course of industrial progress. But by the start of the twentieth
century employers began to take a more tolerant view, accepting the role of
labour relations as a vital part of industrial democracy.

The Post Office, the world's biggest employer, was a civil service
department. It was impossible to settle disputes in such a labyrinthine
organization with employer–employee committees. Instead, all wage
negotiations were carried out by public inquiries, the first being the Post Office
Establishments Committee of 1895, chaired by Lord Tweedmouth – or
'Tweedledum' as some postal colleagues referred to him. But the unions were
poorly represented and the two-year inquiry achieved little, merely stirring up

militancy and work-to-rules. The second two year inquiry, the Businessmen's Committee chaired by Sir Edward Bradford ('Tweedledee') succeeded in securing minor improvements in wages and conditions.

In 1906 the postmaster-general Sydney Buxton set up a Commons Select Committee under the chairmanship of Charles Hobhouse. It attracted wide Press coverage and some concessions for women postal workers. The general view summed up by one of its delegates, E.P.W. Redford, Scottish Post Office secretary, was that 'the majority of post office servants cannot look forward to more than a comparatively subordinate position in life'. It was not very encouraging.

A fourth public inquiry, held between 1912 and 1913 and chaired by Richard Holt, the Liberal MP for Hexham, managed to gain some small pay rises for postal workers and the abolition of good conduct stripes, but it also managed to create an atmosphere of discontent among the Post Office's 176,500 employees.

After the oubreak of the First World War, a committee was set up led by the Liberal MP for Halifax, John Whitley, to find a way to resolve industrial disputes. Its solution was to form joint industrial councils, the Whitley Council for the Post Office being established in 1919. Staffed by post office union representatives, management delegates and independent arbitrators, the Council was to be the GPO's official negotiating body for the next twenty-five years. But it was a civil service compromise and all significant employer–employee negotiations were handled by the new Union of Post Office Workers (UPW).

The UPW, which was formed in 1920, linked all the post office unions for the first time. It was also the largest union in the civil service, with a Cromwell Road mansion as its headquarters and huge rooms with marble fireplaces for each of its twenty principal officers. However, the UPW's early history was overshadowed by the problems of the Great Depression during the 1920s and 1930s, when the government was more interested in gleaning as much money as it could from the GPO than in trying to improve its pay and conditions.

The 'Royal Femail'

One of the most radical causes adopted by the Post Office during the Depression was women's rights. Women were playing a major role in the organization as postmistresses, letter-carriers, savings bank assistants, counter and telegraph clerks and telephone operators, but they continued to be treated as subordinates, and when Rowland Hill seemed to be supporting their cause by employing women as postal clerks, it turned out to be an economic – not philanthropic – gesture. They earned lower wages.

So when women were allowed to work as sorters for the first time, it provoked bitter sarcasm from UPW delegate Jennie Duncan at an annual TUC conference:

> Do women in the post office want equal pay with men? No, oh dear, No! Why not? Oh well, for one thing we aren't quite equal, really, are we? It would be silly to pretend we are, don't you think? Of course it's true that we can do quite well when we are put on the same work and that on the telegraph circuit we often 'whack 'em'; and when we were allowed in the sorting office we had a reputation for high-speed working. But the men never liked it very much; they said we were fools, and seemed to think high-speed sorting done by girls ought to be punishable by death! Seriously, though, we couldn't claim equality, because we don't do night duty. What do you say – 'the men are paid for it'? Well, yes, that's true. But you know it wouldn't be fair to draw the same wages as a man with a wife and family – although it must be admitted he married to please himself, not me.

Jennie Duncan's eloquence seems to have fallen on deaf ears. For when the UPW asked the Post Office to give women child allowances and maternity benefits, the idea was turned down. Whenever a woman postal employee was about to have a baby, she was politely asked to leave the GPO, the Whitley Council pointing out that issues like maternity benefit and equal pay were unsuitable subjects for negotiation. The UPW, however, continued agitating.

With the backing of the other civil service unions, the UPW mounted a propaganada campaign, lobbying Members of Parliament, organising petitions, canvassing the man – and woman – in the street and writing articles for influential newspapers and magazines. They condemned the popular contemporary saying 'A Woman's Place is in the Home' and one agitator, a woman clerk at Camberwell post office, led her colleagues out of the office each night with the refrain:

> I was young when I joined the Branch Committee
> And full of ideas – which was rather a pity,
> For they looked surprised and said to me,
> 'The Clerical Assistant makes the tea!'
> But I vowed I wouldn't remain so meek
> Shouted 'equal pay' and 'the five-day week'
> But they only smiled and said 'Let it be
> The Clerical Assistant makes the tea!

The propaganda took root. In 1936 the government was defeated on a Commons motion on Equal Pay in the Civil Service. The following year the Whitley Council said women employees should be paid 80 per cent of men's wages, but they ruled that women employees could not marry – in case they had children! Jennie Duncan was furious and threatened strike action. And soon she was joined by two formidable allies, the Pankhurst sisters, Sylvia and Christabel, who continued barracking and heckling MPs both inside and outside the House of Commons until in 1944 they wrested a Royal Commission on Equal Pay out of the government.

The Second World War was a marriage of convenience for the women's cause. So many women were needed for emergency postal duties, that the government realized they could no longer ignore them, and in 1946 a government Act allowed married women to work in the Post Office. Ten years later the postwomen's cause reached its climax when women were paid the same as wages as men, provided they too worked in the evenings.

However, the women's movement won a more recent victory in 1985 when the National Union of Civil and Public Servants (NUCAPS) took the case of a hundred senior female nursing staff to tribunal claiming their work was of management status. The tribunal, which was held at Ebury Bridge Road, London, took two-and-a-half years to decide in the women's favour, agreeing in 1987 to a £2,000 a year rise backdated for a year. It was the longest industrial tribunal in history.

Before and After the Second World War

Merger-mania took hold of the unions during the 1930s and 1940s. The first merger attempt occurred when the London Postal Superintending Officers

Association (LPSOA) and Controlling Officers Association (COA) – representing senior managers – tried to link up with the UPW. The move failed due to the superior attitude of the managers' unions. However the two unions later merged with the telegraph supervisors to form the Post Office Management Staffs' Association, which was renamed the Communications Managers Association (CMA). Another merger linked the Association of Civil Service Sorting Assistants (ACSSA) and the Civil Service Clerical Association (CSCA) in 1933.

The Depression had witnessed six postal wage claims, which failed because of the government's obsessive need to keep prices down and the economy stable. Two subsequent claims succeeded however, the GPO adopting a forty hour working week in 1935 and wage rises of 6 to 8 per cent for postal workers in 1938. It proved to be a false dawn. During the Second World War, the government kept wage rises to a minimum, while prices rose 25 per cent. The unions repeatedly lobbied the government to change its mind – but to no avail.

As Britain's post-war economy recovered, so did the Post Office's. In 1951 the dogged UPW won wage rises of almost 10 per cent, and provincial postmen were promoted to the same level as city ones as they cheerfully delivered the mail in their blue summer uniforms. Britain's GPO was positively booming again.

But, as all economists know, booms are followed by troughs and in the 1960s, after the Post Office had dispensed with the Whitley Council, several struggling Conservative and Labour governments turned down one wage claim after another, and when the UPW asked for a 6 per cent rise in 1963, which was refused, it set off a flickering fuse. A total of twenty thousand London postmen walked out of their offices and staged a massive demonstration in Hyde Park. The medicine worked. The government reversed their decision. And, wise after the event, the unions set up the Council for Post Office Unions in 1966 to handle all management negotiations.

In 1969 a Post Office arbitration board was introduced to deal with wage claims. The signs were good, but it proved to be an ominous year for the unions, for it marked the Labour government's White Paper *In Place of Strife*, which reduced several of their powers.

In Times of Strife

Strife or no strife, union hopes were raised when the new Conservative government granted 15 per cent pay rises to the miners, electricity, rail and local government workers. The UPW followed suit, putting in their own 15 per cent claim. But it was turned down. On a freezing cold January day in 1971, the GPO's 180,000 workforce went on strike. Soon post offices, sorting-offices and telephone exchanges were surrounded by squads of angry banner-waving pickets.

However, unknown to the unions, frantic talks had been going on between the UPW general-secretary Tom Jackson and Post Office chairman Sir William Ryland, and days later the strikers were offered rises of 8½ to 10 per cent. They turned them down. The strike was a matter of principle. Other public utility workers had been given 15 per cent pay rises. Why not the Post Office?

Britain was temporarily cut off, with no mail collections or deliveries, and only emergency and STD telephone calls. Hardest hit were the mail order and football pools companies, one mail order firm, Littlewoods, having to lay off six thousand workers; businessmen and chambers of commerce used their own vans and lorries to make deliveries, and to send and pick up orders, contracts and bills; while overseas mail was sent via the Irish Republic; the Dowager Lady Birdwood, a member of the Racial Preservation Society, even set up an alternative post, the Association of Private Postal Services.

The British public took the strike personally. Though one London businessman called it a 'merciful respite from creditors and a cast-iron alibi for unwanted acquaintances', and a *Times* correspondent wrote, 'How blissful is the postman's strike. Business back to simple principles again. No writing acknowledging or confirming orders. No filing, panning or indexing', this was not a general view, and a second *Times* correspondent summed up the public's mood when he said: 'We have already outgrown the Railway Age; are we now outgrowing the Postal Age too? If we want to keep our friendly village postman, we must pay him properly – or else do without him'.

Talks went on daily until management offered an extra 1 per cent. It was rejected, and by the end of February the strike fund had nearly run out, postal workers' families were suffering and morale was at its lowest ebb, though during one Hyde Park rally seven-year-old Kevin Butler went up to Jackson in

Speaker's Corner. The negotiating skills of Tom Jackson, leader of the UPW, brought an early end to the 1971 postal strike. Jackson often referred to the stoppage as 'The Blitz' during his speeches

mid-speech and handed him a hatful of 1,782 pennies for the strikers. After calling several emergency meetings, the strikers held a ballot. On 4 March they voted to go back to work, reluctantly accepting the slightly higher pay offer.

In Times of Peace

During the rest of the 1970s things began to improve. Mechanization boosted Post Office morale, putting less pressure on employees, who suddenly received pay rises, some of them as much as 20 per cent. In 1975 the Equal Pay Act gave women complete equality. And the only major UPW activity in an otherwise peaceful decade occurred at the Grunwick photographic processing factory in London when 137 workers walked out over their management's failure to recognize union status. The UPW pledged their support by blacking all mail to the factory for two years until the dispute ended in 1976.

The role was reversed again in the 1980s. The decade started off well enough when, in 1980, a streamlined UPW changed its name to the Union of Communication Workers (UCW), forming two executive committees for both telephones and post and reinforcing its regional branches. However, it was not long before pay claims were being rejected, working conditions deteriorating and mail volumes growing unwieldy. Then as a last straw, two hundred unofficial strikes shook Post Office management in 1988. The south-east was particularly hard hit. Part-timers were needed in the over-congested sorting-offices, and bonuses were introduced to attract them, a move which upset full-timers who had never been paid bonuses. As a result, the UCW called a national strike in September 1988.

This time the blackout lasted three weeks. Flurries of private couriers with names like The Penny Black and The Last Post started handling mail for high fees, and at least one company asked for a government licence to run an alternative postal service, but without success. After strenuous negotiations, Post Office management agreed to pay bonuses to full-time staff, the strike was called off and peace reigned again.

Led by the UCW, the postal unions have coped with a century of industrial peace and strife. They have striven effectively for better pay and conditions, women's rights and, recently, racial equality. Despite some reduction in their powers, they continue to be articulate and respected postal spokesmen. It is hard to predict what effect privatization will have on them. At first they opposed the idea, forming the Campaign Against the Privatisation of the Post Office (CAPPO) to protect the public monopoly and press for higher wages and aggressive recuitment. But they were in for a pleasant surprise. When one of the Post Office's four key companies, Girobank, was sold to the Alliance and Leicester Building Society in 1990, almost all its jobs, wages and conditions were left untouched by its new private owner.

12
Voices of the People

They also serve who only stand and wait.

John Milton

The Post Office Users National Council

We live in a high-profile consumer society. We know our personal needs, what is on sale, where to buy it and the glossy way in which it is sold. In short we know what is good – and bad – for us and when we think we have been betrayed, we say so, in the Press, on television and the radio and via consumer organizations.

It was with the new consumer in mind that the government set up the Post Office Users National Council (POUNC), under the chairmanship of Lord Peddie, in 1969 – the year the Post Office became a corporation.

People's Champion. Tom Corrigan, chairman of POUNC

POUNC acts as an independent critic of the Post Office, putting pressure on it when it feels it is merited and protecting its many users, or consumers. POUNC's members are recruited by the Department of Trade and Industry from a wide range of specialist professions. It has a London-based secretariat of civil servants, while smaller, satellite POUNCs serve consumers in Scotland, Wales and Northern Ireland.

When the Post Office is proposing changes, such as higher stamp prices or new delivery times, it is statutorily obliged to tell POUNC – or 'Pounce' as it is sometimes known – beforehand. POUNC then issues a report that is published in the media – a sort of buyers' guide for the consumer.

As the vigilante of the man- or woman-in-the-street, POUNC deals with up to nine thousand complaints a year. If a customer has a problem over a lost postal item or what he considers to be unfair treatment by the Post Office, he has two options. The first is to contact POUNC. The second is to approach his local Post Office manager who will try to resolve it for him. If he takes his complaint to POUNC, it will make representations on his behalf and, if necessary, refer the matter to a government arbitration panel.

An independent body, POUNC conducts surveys on a wide variety of Post Office activities. This work is aided by two hundred local Post Office advisory panels, which are sponsored by chambers of commerce and local councils, whose members are non-business people with no vested interest in the Post Office.

One of POUNC's preoccupations is finance. Each year the Post Office contributes a percentage of its profits to the government, who transfers it to government stocks. In 1987 the sum was £93m, in 1990, £91m, and in 1992, £74m. The interest on these stocks is then returned to the Post Office for re-investment. Before it was privatized, the only other nationalized industry to subsidise the government was the Central Electricity Generating Board. British Rail and the Coal Board receive government money instead.

Giving money to the state has been a Post Office tradition for over three hundred years. In 1659 King Charles II asked for money to pay for his mistresses; then in 1685 King James II asked for an annual retainer to be paid to the 'king's purse'; finally it was sanctioned by Act of Parliament in 1711 for the 'settling of a weekly sum out of the Revenues thereof for the Services of the War and for other of Her Majesty's Occasions'. During the Napoleonic Wars, the prime minister Sir William Pitt used Post Office funds to help pay for ships and armaments. It was also used as a funding agency in the Victorian era, and to aid the country's depleted resources during the First and Second World Wars.

This annual contribution is now referred to as the External Financing Limit (EFL) and goes towards the government's Public Sector Borrowing Requirement (PSBR) for spending on defence, the upkeep of roads, housing, the environment and other public services.

For ten years POUNC has campaigned for the EFL to be reduced or removed so that the Post Office can make long-term financial plans without government interference, and spend more on vital new equipment, offices, recruitment and marketing. Thanks to POUNC's efforts, the EFL contributions in 1988 and 1993 were reduced to £57m and £68m, respectively. The Department of Trade and Industry, which periodically issues reports on the Post Office, also recommends a reduction in the EFL.

Delivery Rate

In 1968 the Post Office introduced two-tier posting to speed up mail-sorting. First-class mail was given priority, while less urgent, second-class items were given a longer delivery period. POUNC has studied the progress of first-class mail since it began, issuing statistics on the percentages of next-day deliveries. From 1980 to 1990, the figures rose from 80 to 90 per cent for local first-class letters and from 50 to 60 per cent for long-distance ones. In 1993 long distance deliveries reached 85 per cent and local arrivals 93 per cent. Britain's next-day delivery average was 90 per cent – the highest in Europe.

Both POUNC and the Post Office make postal progress checks. In 1988, after a campaign by POUNC and the Mail Users Association (MUA), a commercial watch-dog, the GPO introduced end-to-end measurement. Trackers from an independent research company checked specified letters, recording where and when they were posted, their progress through the sorting-offices and the time they arrived at their destinations. The same technique was used to monitor inter-city mail flows.

Letter delivery is close to the consumer's heart, as the majority of POUNC's mail testifies. Sometimes customers like to compare today's performances with those before the Second World War, the Victorian era, or the days of William Dockwra's penny post when there were up to twelve deliveries a day in London.

After the post came to a halt during the 1971 and 1988 stoppages, POUNC received several hundred hand-delivered letters seeking the causes of the strikes, how long they were likely to last, and what alternatives might be offered. Many writers said they were disheartened to see one of Britain's most familiar features – the post-box – blocked by an iron bar, one of them pointing out that post-boxes were 'no longer ergonomically-pleasing – merely sources of frustration which foil the customer as he anxiously runs to catch the last delivery and finds the box blocked with a little note underneath'.

Another consumer concern is with circulars and advertising literature. With nearly a billion items sent per year, direct mail – sometimes humorously referred to as 'junk and disorderly' – comprises just over 50 per cent of Britain's postal traffic. POUNC advises customers who do not wish to receive it to contact the Mailing Preference Service (071–738–1625), who will put their names on a special opt-out register.

The Public Eye

Queues, queues, queues, the shopper's daily nightmare, featured in a recent POUNC campaign. The result was most encouraging. For it found that queueing times at post offices are generally shorter than at banks, building societies and supermarkets. The Post Office had a 95 per cent success rate in keeping queues within the magic five minute period. But just in case numbers get out of hand, Crown post offices appoint a member of staff to act as a queue monitor each day.

POUNC also helped introduce training schemes to brighten up the appearance and attitudes of post office counter clerks, who meet more members of the public than the average postman. It has also lobbied successfully for more part-timers at peak times in both post and sorting-offices. In fact, much of the Post Office's high-tech sorting and counter equipment can be part-attributed to POUNC's efforts.

All POUNC's campaigns are aimed at the consumer, whether it be making him more comfortable, speeding up the service he receives, or keeping down the prices he has to pay. In 1982 and 1986 POUNC managed to prevent proposed rises in stamp prices as it believed them unnecessary. Then in 1988 POUNC pressure led to a widespread increase in the number of shops and outlets selling stamps, including petrol stations, newsagents, grocery stores and corner shops. The following year POUNC helped to introduce Sunday collections at twenty thousand British post-boxes. It also campaigned for the use of the postcode on all mail items and persuaded British Telecom to include subscribers' postcodes in telephone directories. One of its most successful efforts was to persude the Post Office to create community post offices in remote areas.

Mail Users Association

Many consumer-related companies dealing in mail order, marketing and the football pools depend on the Post Office; others, such as financial institutions, banks, publishing companies, charities, advertising and public relations agencies find it an invaluable source of revenue. Like consumers, companies must also have their people's champions to protect their interests.

One day in the summer of 1974, Julian Blackwell, chairman of Blackwells, the booksellers, was visiting a cricket match at Lord's when an idea came to him. He jotted his thoughts down on a piece of paper, propped up on his car bonnet, and then contacted a close friend, Robin Fairlie, a director of the Readers Digest Association. Together the two men drafted the first constitution of the Mail Users Association – a commercial version of POUNC.

The MUA is based in London with a small full-time staff. It has more than two hundred member-companies who pay an annual registration fee averaging £450. For this the MUA makes representations on their behalf and lobbies the Post Office as and when it thinks fit. Its aim is to ensure the GPO 'stays healthy and vigorous and serves its industrial, commercial and institutional users properly.'

Like POUNC, the MUA has run a number of mail campaigns. Recently it agitated companies to improve training in post-rooms, to make sure employees – whether supervisors, secretaries, or post-room assistants – learnt the correct way to sort, process and package outgoing mail. The introduction of the Post Office's Mailsort scheme in 1988 was partly due to the MUA's efforts. It means that companies which pre-sort four thousand or more first-class items qualify for a postal discount of up to 14 per cent, plus an extra 2 per cent before 1.00 p.m. At least 90 per cent of the sorted letters must have postcodes. For less time-sensitive items such as mail-circulars, price lists, reports and direct mail, companies can qualify for up to 32 per cent off the standard postage. The MUA also helped introduce the Postcode Project. Companies sending out more than twenty thousand items a day qualify for financial aid towards the cost of their postcoding equipment.

Another MUA campaign helped to introduce Datapost, a same-day parcel delivery service with a money-back guarantee. If a parcel fails to arrive on time, the Post Office refunds the postage. The same applies to international Datapost and Swiftair letter schemes.

The MUA fights hard for its member-companies. When the GPO announced it was raising parcel prices by 25 per cent, the MUA and the Union of Communications Workers (UCW) successfully lobbied the Post Office to keep the increase down to 12½ per cent. And when the Post Office said it was introducing a 25p 'Superstamp' to guarantee next-day delivery in the 1980s, the MUA successfully fought against it, arguing that it would merely do what a first-class stamp was supposed to do already – at a higher price.

Association of Mail Order Publishers

Leisure publishing has taken off in the past few years, with tens of thousands of British companies selling videos, sending books and pictures to people's homes, and running CD, video and record clubs, newsletters and magazines. In 1970 the Association of Mail Order Publishers (AMOP) was set up to represent what it described as 'the cinderellas of the advertising world'. To join AMOP a company must have a postal turnover of £46m plus per year. In return, AMOP protects its members' interests, acts as a pressure group and leads postal campaigns. In 1989 AMOP and the MUA produced a joint report, 'Deliver Us from the Post Office', in which they suggested that all GPO services be sub-contracted to private firms.

Watchdogs such as POUNC, the MUA and AMOP can only influence; they cannot change, or legislate for, organizations. Their job is to monitor the Post Office's performance and defend their members' rights, which they will continue to do so long as it remains in its present form.

Private View of a Public Service

Early in 1993 serious talk about privatization began rumbling round the House of Commons and Post Office headquarters. Private posts, however, are nothing new. The first one carried letters for the public in the fifteenth century, the last for Oxford and Cambridge University students until it was banned for 'unofficial and illegal' carrying by postmaster-general Lord Manners in 1886.

Rumours of the the Post Office being privatised have been raised and resisted since the 1970s, mainly because of the indignity of having a Royal Mail without the king's or queen's head on its stamps. Strong Conservative lobbies have agitated for reform, and in 1988 Conservative MPs John Bowis and Theresa Gorman introduced pro-privatization private member's bills. The following year the Adam Smith Institute, a right-wing pressure group, said in a report:

> If we want a postal system that is enterprising and responsive to changing private demand and not subject to continual disruption then we must remove the ancient and anachronistic Post Office monopoly. This should not be done as an act of blind faith in the benevolent, invisible hands of potential private postmen, but as a conscious policy of liberating a key area of the economy from a restrictive regime that owes its existence to civil war paranoia, its continuation to government greed and its survival to political inertia.

Courier companies like DataExpress, Securicor and DHL International have tried to introduce private postal networks and, in 1989, the Australian-based TNT applied for a government licence to run an alternative post which was turned down. Even the Post Office itself has moved towards privatization. In 1981 the Post Office Act not only converted the GPO's telephone service into British Telecom, which went private in 1984, it also reduced the GPO's monopoly by allowing private carriers to take postal items costing more than £1. In 1986 a further Post Office Act divided the GPO into four separate businesses, Girobank, Post Office Counters, Royal Mail Letters and Post Office Parcels (Parcelforce), and in 1987 Post Office Counters became a limited company to allow it to compete more effectively on the open market. Finally, in 1990 Girobank went private when it was sold to the Alliance and Leicester building society for £111.9m.

In the past ten years nationalized industries such as gas, water and electricity have been sold to the private sector, with British Rail about to go the same way. Now, for political, electoral, and financial reasons, the Post Office has been spearheaded for privatization over the next five years. If the government sells the whole network, it will raise about £2 billion, but lose about £170 million a year in public sector contributions. However, the actual structure of a private Post Office will depend on political priorities in a highly labour-intensive organization employing more than two hundred thousand people.

The plan has undoubted merits. First, despite Parcelforce's impressive record, a large multi-carrier service would relieve letter and parcel congestion on inter-city and major town routes. Second, by losing its government tie, the Post Office will be able to make five year plans and spend more of its profits on capital investment, recruitment and advertising.

On the other hand, a private network would end the post's royal status, remove one of Britain's last remaining public services and destroy the image of the friendly local postman. It might also raise stamp prices to pay for post in rural areas which currently lose the Post Office more than £20m a year.

We will, however, have to leave such musings to the laws of free enterprise.

13
The Men of Secrets

Proper officers are quietly watching in the quarters suspected.

Post Office memorandum, 1793

The Glasgow Night Express was making its weekly run to London on Friday 3 August 1963, when just outside Oxford the driver noticed one of the trackside signals showing red instead of green. He slowed the train to a halt and leant out of his cab to see if there was anything blocking the track; the driver's mate, meanwhile, went to the back of the engine-cab to make a routine check on the air pressure. They heard footsteps and suddenly two men wearing balaclavas jumped onto the engine footplate and into the cab, overpowering the driver and mate, and tying them up. It was the start of the biggest rail hold-up in history – The Great Train Robbery.

The robbery led to a massive international manhunt. Police forces all over the south-east of England set up special operations rooms; security on mail trains was tightened and all rail coaches were fitted with short-wave emergency radios; helicopters scoured the countryside for traces of the robbers; and, as the hunt spread, police forces on the continent joined the widening net.

The tell-tale phrase 'don't move for half-an-hour' uttered by one of the robbers to train driver Jack Mills convinced the police that their hide-out was nearby and led them to Leatherslade Farm, Buckinghamshire, 30 miles from the hold-up. The robbers had made a hurried exit, but police were able to trace fingerprints on personal possessions dropped during the getaway . . . clues which eventually led to the first two arrests in Bournemouth several weeks later.

Two of the men seconded to the Scotland Yard robbery squad and the investigation headquarters at Aylesbury were Ron Woodward and Harry Lyons, of the Post Office Investigation Department.

The POID – or ID as it is popularly known – is a small band of three hundred men, based at Croyden, Surrey, who act as the Post Office's detectives. They do not wear uniforms or hold ranks and are all regarded as equal. Their job is to police the daily activities of the Post Office, to investigate crimes and try to prevent them happening. The ID detectives usually work in twos or threes ready to be called to any part of the country where a crime has been reported.

Their motto is *Suaviter in modo, fortiter in re* (subtle in method, vigorous in deed). They also need tact and discretion in their work as they are dealing with fellow employees in an organization of more than two hundred thousand. To aid investigations, the ID has about fifty associates, all of whom work in the Post Office and have signed the Official Secrets Act. It is their job to tip off the ID whenever they see anything suspicious.

If an ID detective suspects a postal employee of a misdemeanour, he takes him to a private room and interviews him together with another ID member. The ID always tries to be as fair as possible, its code being that an employee is innocent until proved guilty. Any suspect employee can therefore bring a friend or colleague with him to interviews. If the suspicions are groundless, the employee will be allowed to go back to work as usual. If he has committed a minor offence, the employee is warned or disciplined by his manager. If the offence is more serious, such as money-letter theft or fraud, he will be suspended from duty, arrested and dealt with by the criminal courts.

The ID detective does not have the policeman's powers of arrest; like any other member of the public, he can make a citizen's arrest, but for a legal arrest, he must go through a member of the ID's team of ten solicitors. This means that his evidence must be foolproof, and, in 1987 ID detectives began using a technique that even surpassed the police force's top brains. A group of researchers pointed out that it would be far easier to tape-record interviews and thus give a foolproof version of what was said, rather than write them down which was nearly always subject to error. So instead of notebooks, detectives brought tape-recorders to interviews. It meant that when an ID detective had to make an arrest or appear in court, his evidence was completely watertight and could not be challenged by either the suspect, his solicitor, or the defence. A grateful police force adopted the idea two years later.

Many ID detectives are ex-policemen. Both its recent general manager and the present head of laboratories are former CID commanders. There are no women in the male-oriented ID and, like all teams of detectives and investigators, it has a slightly macabre sense of humour. Members always chuckle at any mention of their nickname: 'The G-Men of the GPO'.

Most of the crimes the ID handles are internal, involving money-letter theft or fraud syndicates. Investigations must be discreet, and in such a large network can be very time-consuming. ID members sometimes face months of silent detective-work and painstaking inquiries in several regions before coming up with any clues. To aid its inquiries, the ID has forensic laboratories and teams of fingerprint and handwriting experts at its main London office in Aldersgate Street. It also has a research department where detectives can follow up leads and clues, collect evidence and develop new techniques such as the tape-recording of interviews.

Apart from money-letter thefts, the three biggest Post Office crimes are mail-van robberies, mail-train hold-ups and National Savings Bank frauds. The ID has three specialist departments at Aldersgate Street that deal only in these crimes. The police force also help out in some cases, though an embarrassing mix-up occurred when both forces were called to the scene of an armed £½m mail-van hold-up in Twickenham, Middlesex. Seeing two men dashing down a High Street alley, the police gave chase, and finally brought them to the ground, only to find they had captured two ID detectives. The red-faced CID detectives offered their apologies, and the two teams resumed the chase together, successfully catching the escaping robbers.

One little-known fact is that the ID was founded before the police force. Started in 1793, it is the oldest team of investigators in the United Kingdom, and the second in the world after the USA's customs and excise investigation department. ID detectives were investigating crimes twelve years before the Bow Street Runners started policing London's streets, thirty-six years before Sir Robert Peel founded the Metropolitan Police, and eighty-five years before the CID was set up in 1878.

A small group of ID detectives was first used at the Post Office's main sorting-office in Lombard Street, London, by secretary Francis Freeling, after a government committee had reported a disturbing outbreak of money-letter thefts. Several weeks later, Freeling told the postmaster-general, the Earl of Walsingham:

Proper officers are quietly watching in the quarters suspected, with the hope that if depradations are really committed by people in your Lordship's employ, some discovery can be made.

Freeling then appointed London solicitor Anthony Parkin, to prosecute highwaymen, fraudsters and thieves caught stealing banknotes and bills of exchange from clerks, sorters and letter-carriers.

But to trace the origins of the ID we have to go back to the Post's first-known elements of corruption – the roguish innkeeper-postmasters of the seventeenth-century, who stole the contents of money-letters, and their protégés, the young, feckless post-boys, who often fell into bad company at local inns and taverns and stole from mail-bags, which gave rise to the saying 'Crooked as a post-boy'.

Despite the efforts of successive masters of the post, these costly practices carried on unheeded until the start of the eighteenth century. Enter Ralph 'the reformer' Allen. In 1720 Allen, the master of the posts, appointed three surveyors to spy on innkeepers and to stop and search post-boys on the highways. These two measures helped reduce money-letter thefts, which in 1750 became a hanging offence. Allen's successor, John Palmer, was another innovator. He introduced the streamlined stage-coach, but had not reckoned with a dark presence that emerged to taunt the passengers of the new carriages. Highwaymen like Dick Turpin held up and sometimes shot stage-coach drivers with blunderbusses before forcing the frightened passengers to hand over their valuables and postal packets (see Chapter 3). But, like Allen, Palmer was not to be outdone. He appointed armed guards to sit over the mail at the rear of the stage-coaches, and one by one the posses of highwaymen disappeared, the robberies stopped, and Britain's letter-writing public heaved a huge sigh of relief.

At the start of the nineteenth century, Post Office management was faced with a more sophisticated crime. Illegal franking – or forging MPs' signatures on the backs of letters to qualify for free postage – had become a popular pastime among the more literary members of the public (see Chapter 4). One of the most notorious perpetrators of this crime was a London forger named John Hatfield. His infamy led to Britain's first wanted posters, put up in 1802 and offering £50 reward for his capture. That same year *The Times* reported:

> Saturday last, a young fellow who calls himself Edward Moorin was committed to New Prison by Sir J. Fielding for the forging and uttering of counterfeit franks, when it appeared that he had put off, mostly at coffee-houses, upwards of 1,200 dozen by which he had received about

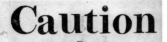

Cautionary Tale. A series of posters that were displayed during Sir Francis Freeling's postal security drive

250 pounds ready money, the price he sold them at being from 4s. to 6s. per dozen.

Illegal franking was finally banned in 1840.

Money-letter thefts were the Post Office's *bête noire*. Freeling often warned his employees of the 'awful example of the consequences of suppressing any letters.' One of the last offenders to hang for money-letter theft was Arthur Baily in 1811. Baily was born and brought up in Ashburton, Devon and, at the age of fourteen, moved with his parents to Bath, where he got a job as a sorter at the town's main post office. After seven years at the sorting-office, Baily left to marry a local girl, after which he bought a pub in the town where the couple lived and worked, managing to bring up six children at the same time. However, whenever Bath post office was short-staffed during peak periods or at Christmas-time, Baily would help out with the afternoon sorting. One day during the summer of 1811, he was helping to fill one of the postmen's sacks when he was seen opening a money-letter, taking out a credit note payable to Messrs Slack, a Bath firm of linen drapers, and signing the back so that he could cash it at the local bank. Baily was reported to the authorities, interviewed and arrested. After admitting a series of similar thefts, he was sent for trial and sentenced to hang.

On 11 September 1811 Baily was taken by horse and cart from Bath prison to the gallows at nearby Ilcester. As he mounted the scaffold, the 37-year-old postman, who was holding a prayer-book in his right hand, said to the assembled crowd:

> I hope you will take warning – I hope and beg you to look often into this book, and you will not come to shame. Be sure to be honest, and not covet money, cursed money! and particularly money that is not your own.

The last letter-carrier to be hanged was John Barrett who was sent to the gallows at Newgate Prison on 13 February 1832. Three years later hanging for letter-theft was abolished. The maximum penalty for the offence was a seven year deportation order to Australia.

However, such thefts continued to lose the Post Office three-quarters of its revenue. As a result it went on security alert. In 1837 police constables with tipstaffs were appointed to watch over the busier sorting-offices, while a Bow

Empty Gesture. A robber is foiled in his attempt to steal money-letters from a mail-coach in 1843

Street Runner was paid a guinea a week to guard St Martin's-le-Grand's large courtyard where mail was loaded on to outgoing stage-coaches. The same year, teams of travelling officers were assigned to follow up missing letters from their place of posting to their reported loss, interviewing members of the public and postal employees and, if necessary, making citizen's arrests. These tough measures helped recoup some of the Post Office's dwindling revenue.

After the Penny Post, security was treated even more seriously. In 1843 a team of twenty-two detectives, known as the 'Confidential Bureau', started policing the sorting-offices and following up cunning crimes in the national network. Headed by John Ramsey, the Bureau worked closely with the police during major investigations and the police also helped to guard the recently opened savings banks, which had become prey to large-scale savings book forgeries by European syndicates.

To help crack the syndicates, the Bureau recruited detectives who could speak foreign languages. They had some success, but languages or no languages, savings bank forgeries were one of the Post Office's main headaches for many years.

In 1861 the Bureau changed its name to the Investigation Branch (the IB), and in keeping with its more authoratitive title, found a new way to help curb money-letter theft. A researcher who had been working on methods of crime prevention came up with the idea of test letters. Whenever theft was suspected at a sorting-office, replicas of missing money-letters – test letters – would be posted into the system. Then a detective would wait in a secret hide-out at the sorting area and watch the sorters at work. If he saw an employee opening one of the letters, he was able to catch him red-handed. As a result, the IB were able to arrest many of the culprits and help reduce the spate of thefts. The test-letter proved so successful that it is still used by postal detectives.

The inventive IB then came up with another deterrent – the watching-gallery. Detectives were able to spy on sorters by suspending hideaways – or watching-galleries – over sorting areas. As with test letters, it meant they were able to see sorters breaking the law and arrest them on the spot. Watching-galleries are still used for sorting-office surveillance, though recently many of them have been replaced by small closed circuit televisions.

By the end of the nineteenth century the IB had a team of fifty detectives or, as their colleagues were fond of describing them, Men of Secrets.

The Train Robbers

With the advent of steam, train robbers replaced highwaymen as the scourge of the Post Office. In 1922 two famous hold-ups captured the public's, if not the Investigation Branch's, imagination. Just after the New Year, the Antwerp to London mail train was nearing London when it was boarded by robbers. Breaking into the mail-van, they held the postmen-guards at gunpoint and escaped with £80,000 of bonds. A six year hunt proved fruitless until, in 1928, an East End bank manager found a series of suspicious-looking serial numbers on a collection of bonds held by one of his customers. The matter was put in the hands of the IB, who found the suspect numbers tallied with those on the stolen bonds, and discovered that the customer, a respected solicitor, was the robbery's mastermind. He was arrested and jailed for five years.

The second hold-up occurred as the London to Bradford Night Express was approaching Bradford. Four robbers climbed along the outside and broke into the mail-van, overpowering the guard and escaping with three registered GPO bags containing £17,000. Having escaped with their booty, the robbers couldn't decide what to do with it, and hid it near a brewery in the Bradford suburbs. A few days later, a man walking his dog discovered the stolen sacks. He reported his find to the IB, who put a twenty-four hour watch on the site. Two days later one of the robbers came back for the sacks. He was caught red-handed by the IB and he and his accomplices were sent to prison.

The Birmingham Phone Bug

Another common twentieth-century crime was telephone-tapping or bugging, perhaps the most unusual case being the Tale of The Birmingham Phone Bug. For several months an operator at Birmingham telephone exchange had been seen listening to police callers' conversations, taking down details of crimes and making a tidy income by selling them to the Birmingham newspapers. An IB detective with a talent for mimicry phoned one day and spun a remarkable yarn. In his best Scots' accent he claimed he was a lorry driver who had been hired by a Scottish landowner to fetch a herd of rare Chinese deer from Birmingham airport. After picking up the deer, he had been driving back to Scotland when, during a blizzard, his lorry got stuck in a snowdrift and the deer escaped. He asked the Birmingham police – whom he had already alerted about the hoax – to send out a search-party. Then he rang off. Watched by a second IB detective, the greedy operator then phoned all the Birmingham newspapers. But they too had been tipped off about the story, and it proved to be his swan-song.

Doing the Lambeth Walk

During the Second World War, IB work was classed as a reserved occupation. Because of their postal crime prevention responsibilities, detectives were not allowed to join the armed forces. After the war, the Branch had a large team of 150 detectives and a small group of associates who tipped them off whenever their suspicions were aroused. It was one such tip-off that led to the case of the Lazy Postman of Lambeth.

At 6.30 each morning a young postman would leave Lambeth sorting-office for his first delivery, returning mid-morning for a tea-break, before going out on his second round. Just after 1.00 one afternoon, an IB associate – who lived on the postman's south London round – spotted him getting out of his car in Milton Keynes. Suspicious that he should have strayed so far from home, the associate phoned IB headquarters. A few days later the postman was seen by another associate in High Wycombe. This time he was standing by a post-box, taking letters out of a sack and posting them. Again the incident was reported to the IB. Investigators later discovered that, instead of going out on his second deliveries, the lazy postman had been visiting friends and re-posting the letters he should have been delivering on his Lambeth walk. The lazy postman was suspended from duty. However, if he had been caught doing such a thing in the nineteenth century, he would have been sent to prison for 'betraying his position in a place of trust'.

The Butcher and the Betting Slip

The betting laws played havoc with the postal service in the 1950s and 1960s. There were few betting shops and people who liked to have a wager on the horses or dogs were allowed to send their bets by post. Then a number of clever postmen started abusing the system.

In 1962 a butcher from Battersea, London, had a series of large racing wins, including a £150,000 bonanza on a seven-horse tote at Pontefract. The bookie who received the postal bets became suspicious and contacted the IB. A few days later an IB detective came and interviewed the butcher, and when he asked him to sign his name, found it differed from the one on the £150,000 betting-slip. The butcher explained that he had been in a hurry that day and had asked a friend in his local pub to sign it for him. The detective didn't believe him, and asked a local police detective to help him with the case. The man from the CID said he recognized the signature on the betting-slip as that of a local postman and said he knew the butcher and postman were friends. The IB detective went to the pub, where he found the postman who, after being arrested, admitted he had filled in the betting-slips after the races, and before posting them, had put the envelopes through a franking-machine to show the previous day's date. It meant that when the bookies received them, they appeared to be quite legitimate. The two men were sent to prison, and after that, postal betting was banned for members of the Post Office.

The Trojan Horse

In 1972 the IB became the ID, or the Investigation Division. But not only did it have new name, the ID also found it had got a new crime to deal with. The Case of the Trojan Horse began at Euston station when the last sacks of mail were being loaded on to the London to Manchester Night Express. Suddenly a very flustered young woman ran down the platform towing two large wooden trunks behind her. Pointing out that she was an actress appearing in a play at the Manchester Exchange Theatre the next evening, she said the trunks carried a large number of costumes that were needed for the rest of the cast. The helpful sorters duly loaded them into the guard's van.

The train set off on its long journey, and was making its way through Watford, when one of the passengers, who happened to be a member of the ID, became suspicious of the woman and her two trunks, and leaving his carriage, strolled down to the guard's van where he asked if he might open one of the trunks. He did so, and to his surprise, found a man wearing an oxygen mask attached to a cylinder inside. When, with the guard's permission, he opened the second trunk he found it filled with banknotes. Apparently, when the guard and two sorters had left the guard's van for a tea-break, the man, who had been watching them through a peephole, climbed out of his Trojan Horse and emptied the contents of a white registered mail-bag into the other trunk, before climbing back again. The robber, who was a former postman, had been planning to divide the spoils with his female accomplice in Manchester. However, unlike the wily Greeks who successfully entered Troy hidden in a Trojan Horse, the modern version of the story was foiled.

Crime and Punishment

The number of Post Office investigations rose so fast in the 1960s, that in 1972 the ID left the Post Office and joined the Department of Trade and Industry. It was, if you like, becoming too close to its client. By having its own headquarters and regional bases, the ID could take a more detached role in postal investigations and also work on cases for the police, customs and airport authorities and company investigators.

In 1973 the ID started giving courses on crime prevention and security for the CID, security firms and company personnel departments. With the backing of the Post Office, it also set up a crime prevention degree course at Cranfield Institute of Technology, Bedford. The ID found its main preoccupation was computer bugging – or the illegal tapping of computer systems – and thefts of top-security computer data, two crimes that cost banks, financial institutions and the GPO billions of pounds a year.

The ID also sells many of its security devices overseas. One of them – the Interceptor – has helped cope with the most dangerous Post Office crime of the past two decades – letter-bombs. The bombs, most of which are sent by terrorists or political extremists, usually target MPs or public figures. As a result, the Post Office carries out stringent checks on all mail bound for the Houses of Parliament or prominent people. If a suspect letter-bomb is discovered, the Interceptor, a reinforced plastic cylinder, is placed over it. The device, which can contain the blast from a 2 lb bomb, is particularly useful when a bomb is found in a dangerous or exposed public place, and enables ID detectives to prevent an explosion until the police bomb squad arrive. Another ID invention, a sealed letter-box called the Mailsafe, has helped reduce the rise in letter-box arson on housing estates. The Mailsafe, which has foiled more than five thousand arson attacks, releases a heavy gas if any lighted object is placed inside, rapidly extinguishing it.

The Men of Secrets

The Men of Secrets find they have to live up to their reputation when dealing with the press. Whenever there is a big postal crime, detectives are reluctant to talk to reporters or show films or videos of the incident to protect their patron, the Post Office. Any publicity would give robbers ideas about the postal network and lead to copycat crimes. For that reason, details of most armed mail-van robberies, post office raids, and train hold-ups never appear in the press, radio and television. After the Great Train Robbery, the ID refused to give out information about new security devices being fitted to mail-trains for fear of a repeat of the £2.6m crime, though, ironically, the robbery's elusive mastermind is thought to have been a Post Office employee.

Bomb Prevention. The Interceptor, a reinforced plastic cylinder, is used by the Investigation Division to prevent letter-bomb explosions

Fire Prevention. A letter-box known as a Mailsafe is used to combat arson attacks on vulnerable housing estates

14
The Hobby of Kings

A bit of paper . . . covered at the back with a glutinous wash.
Rowland Hill, Post Office Reform, 1837

Victorian ladies of leisure who liked to pass the time in quiet contemplation were the world's first stamp-collectors. *Punch* duly noted in 1842:

A new mania has bitten the industriously idle ladies of England. . . .
They betray more anxiety to treasure up Queen's heads than Harry the
Eighth did to get rid of them.

Then on 29 October 1842, an advertisement appeared in *The Times* from a young lady who wished to 'cover my dressing-room with cancelled [used] postage stamps'.

However, in 1842 lady collectors had a limited range to choose from. There was the Penny Black, the Twopenny Blue, the Penny Red and one or two miscellaneous issues, and they all had just one common feature – Queen Victoria's head. The postage stamp had not yet caught on overseas, the first country to adopt it being Brazil in 1843. The Germans were next to consider the 'pretty little pictures', followed by France, and in 1845 the USA, after a big reduction in postal rates.

By 1854 twenty-one countries were using stamps, most of which bore the head of the reigning king or queen. That year Rowland Hill, the Penny Black pioneer, was able to report to the Treasury: 'My plan has been adopted more or less completely by every considerable state in Europe.'

It only took a short time for stamp collecting, or timbromanie as it was known, to become a serious hobby. The first important collector was Edward Stanley Gibbons, founder of the famous stamp firm, who began collecting at school in 1854 and two years later used a window of his father's chemists shop in Plymouth to display and deal in his specimens. Another leading collector was Charles Phillips, who took up timbromanie in 1863, describing it as 'The

Early Starter. Edward Stanley Gibbons began
displaying stamps in a window of his father's
Plymouth chemists shop

King of Hobbies and the Hobby of Kings'. He later bought Edward Stanley
Gibbons' firm and turned it into a limited company.

However, the first nation to be ensnared by the passion was France, where
stamp collecting was studied with the ardour of the French lover. Specimens
were categorized according to quality, condition, size, cost and country, and
shown at private viewings where aristocrats mingled with select circles of
timbromanists. By 1861 the world's first catalogues were being produced in
Paris.

One of the first British collectors was Queen Victoria, who always had a
fascination and respect for the Post Office and the postal system, and, unlike
any other British monarch before or since, always paid for her stamps. She
began her collection in a secret room at Buckingham Palace in 1864, and her
enthusiasm fired her grandson, later King George V, into the philatelic fad. In
1896, he became president of the London Philatelic Society, now known as the
Royal Philatelic Society. King George VI, also a keen collector, continued his
father's role as president, followed in 1953 by our present queen, who each
year shows a selection of royal specimens at the Royal Philatelic Society's
opening meeting.

A Sailor of Fortune

Twentieth-century stamp collecting can be an expensive art. An issue of thirty-six Penny Blacks, which was sold for £525 in 1934, was re-sold in 1989 for £308,000. Today Penny Blacks regularly fetch five figure sums. A recent one with no perforations was sold at Phillips, the auctioneers, for £30,000.

Two of the earliest colonial stamps were the 1847 Penny Red and Twopenny Blue of Mauritius. Later the island issued its own Penny Blacks, and during renovation work at the bishop's palace in the 1950s, workmen found a Penny Black in the foundations. It raised such a good price, that the Mauritian government paid for the rest of the renovation from the proceeds.

In 1856 another colony, British Guiana, produced just two versions of the one cent Magenta. Nothing was heard of the specimens until the 1920s when one of them fell into the hands of an excited Dover schoolboy. He was admiring his new find in a local cafe when it caught the eye of a sailor at a nearby table. The sailor, who was an enthusiastic collector, bought it from him for 3d. Knowing it was only one of two British Guiana Magentas ever issued, the sailor decided to try and trace the owner of the other one, eventually tracking him down to a small town in Texas. The sailor then sold him the stamp for £7,000. However, its new American owner decided to alter philatelic history by burning the other Magenta, thus making the new one unique, and selling it for £12,000.

The Stamp of Success

The world's largest stamp collection is held at the British Library in London, where visitors can view eight million specimens and twenty thousand volumes of literature on philately. Perhaps the Library's finest and best-preserved collection is that of Thomas Tapling, the Victorian MP, who collected every British specimen and nearly every world issue during the fifty years after the Penny Black, including the rare Gold Coast Penny stamp of 1883 and two Hawaiian stamps issued in 1851–2.

However, the largest individual stamp collection in the world is that of Reginald Phillips. His collection, which features mainly nineteenth-century issues, is reputed to be worth more than £1m, and was presented to the National Postal Museum when it opened in King Edward Street, London, in

Rare Specimens. Two of the first colonial stamps were the 1847 Penny Red (above) and Twopenny Blue (below) issued by the island of Mauritius

1966. As a tribute to the collector, the Museum started a Reginald Phillips award scheme for original stamp design in 1969.

Designer Stamps

To its keepers, the stamp is an object of rare beauty and delight; it is said that one in twelve of the British population has collected stamps at some stage of his or her life. Though Rowland Hill was able to dismiss the Penny Black as a thing of 'less than aesthetic appeal', stamp design has become a fine art and each new issue is commissioned from specialist designers.

Stamps have a flair for capturing scenes from almost every walk of life, be it the investiture of the Prince of Wales, British success in football's World Cup, or the 1991 series of roses designed and engraved by artist Yvonne Skargon. Like bird-watching, model-making and brass-rubbing, stamp-collecting is a passion, and one that has led to deeds of derring-do, duels at dawn, and inspired stamp collectors to travel round the world and back in their search for a rare issue. In 1930 war broke out between Paraguay and Bolivia after the two South American countries issued stamps laying claim to the same piece of land.

The Brown Affair

Designing a new stamp issue is a rare gift. When the Post Office needs a new one, it often holds a competition between a number of well-known artists and the standard can be notoriously high.

As a *Times* leader pointed out in September 1937, 'There are many artists, eminent in their own field, who are quite incapable of designing a good postage stamp . . . without irrelevant verbal detail and otiose ornament.' However, on 13 February 1936 a brave schoolboy named Hubert J. Brown from Devon, wrote to the Post Office, asking if he could design a series to mark the ten month reign of King Edward VIII.

The Post Office agreed. So Brown excitedly set to work, making a simple pencil drawing of the King's left profile based on a picture taken by the photographer Hugh Cecil. He sent it to the Post Office on 4 April.

Brown heard no more about his design until 1 September, the date of the new issue. To his surprise and delight, the four stamps commemorating the king's short reign were similar to the one he had contributed. However, instead of a congratulatory telegram, Brown had a letter from the postmaster-general's secretary, Hastings Lees-Smith, which said:

> I am directed by the postmaster-general to your letter of April 4 with which you enclosed a drawing for a suggested postage stamp of the new reign. . . . Stamps of the new reign will appear shortly, and you will see that the design which has been selected bears some features in common with that which you suggested.

The new issue was well received, and Brown was praised by fellow artists for his originality and clever use of detail, but he was upset by the Post Office's grudging attitude. As a result, his father wrote a letter to the postmaster-general expressing the family's disappointment. But the Browns never received a word of reply or explanation from the Post Office.

The Brown affair sparked a fiery debate in *The Times*, which ended with an angry letter from the painter William Rothenstein:

> If no artist today can be trusted to design a decent postage stamp, let the Government at least be honest in the economy and shut up our schools of

art, our national galleries and museums, these costly institutions having, in their eyes, proved useless.

The Stamp that Never Was

Shortly after Germany's invasion of France in 1940, the centenary of the Penny Black, the world's leading stamp nations, Britain and France, decided to produce a stamp to use as a joint propaganda weapon against Germany.

They produced a number of drafts, most of which showed dual portraits of the British king and the French president. However they could not decide which one to use. So the French and English designers went back to work, producing many new ones in varying styles and colours. But they still failed to agree, and the issue deadline of 2 September was drawing near. Then on 17 June news reached GPO headquarters that the Germans had invaded Paris and France had fallen. The French were now under German rule, which meant the joint stamp was now irrelevant. The project was abandoned.

Counterfeit Stamps

War has caused carnage, death and despair. It has also created the world's most evil stamps. During preparations for the Second World War, the Germans made copies of stamps issued to commemorate King George V's silver jubilee, substituting the king's head for that of Joseph Stalin, the Russian leader. They then used the stamp as a ploy to frighten the Allies into believing Russia had conquered Great Britain. In 1937 they continued their propaganda war by copying a stamp featuring the coronation of King George VI, and inserting Joseph Stalin's head instead of the king's wife, Queen Elizabeth. Again they were trying to frighten the Allies into thinking there had been a Russian invasion.

When the war began, the Germans ordered prisoners-of-war who had previously worked as printers to produce counterfeit stamps with cruel messages, at Sachsenhausen concentration camp in Germany. However, Britain retaliated with her own series of counterfeits. The most successful was a stamp showing Hitler's deputy, Heinrich Himmler, interposed over the Führer's head to scare the German people into thinking Hitler had been overthrown and Himmler had taken over as German ruler. The stamps were put on letters snatched from raids on German trains and dropped by aeroplanes or secret agents in batches behind enemy lines. Another British counterfeit showed the picture of a dictatorial Himmler chaining together the German people like a row of captives. One of the cruellest counterfeits, however, was produced by the USA. Called the Death's Head, it featured Hitler as half-man, half-skeleton, while the US-made Spitler stamp showed a little girl spitting in the Führer's face.

A Dietary Tip

Britain produces an average of ten stamp issues a year, and as the founder-nation, does not have to show their country of origin. The world's leading stamp producer, however, is Russia with a hundred and fifty a year, while Brazil makes only four. The world's smallest stamp, one-third of an inch square, was issued by Columbia in 1863; the largest, which measured 8 in by $2^{1}/_{2}$ in, was used on express letters by the Chinese from 1905–12.

One feature of the stamp that never changes, whatever the country, size or denomination, is the 'glutinous wash' on the back. But even that has unexpected properties, according to one firm. In 1990 the American Research Institute warned its female staff in a memo: 'Remember that next time you use a postage stamp, the glue on the back contains one-tenth of a calorie.'

15

The Scarlet Empire

*All history proves the close connection between progress, power and
communications . . . the strength of the British Empire depends upon
good communications.*

Department of Civil Aviation memorandum (1921)

Britain discarded her image as a nation of shopkeepers and became a world
communicator in the twentieth century. She was trading with more than ten
countries and running a large commonwealth. At home, service industries such
as coal, the railways and electricity were flourishing. Not forgetting the Post
Office, of course. In middle-class homes, the telephone was coveted as highly
as the typewriter, gramophone and petrol-driven motor car; letter-writing had
become an endearing source of contact between absent friends; every home
had at least three weekly postal deliveries; inter-company mail was a vital
source of new business; the postman was as familiar a figure-in-the-street as
the policeman; more than thirty-two thousand post-boxes and twenty-two
thousand post offices adorned cities, towns and villages; and the Post Office
was making an annual profit of £12m a year. In short, Britain and her Post
Office were thriving as never before.

There was also an international boom in trade and communications. More
than eighty countries had postal systems and an influential Universal Postal
Union (UPU) to fight for them. Not surprisingly they started to campaign for
cheaper postage. The leader of the British movement was the Conservative MP
John Henniker Heaton, creator of the commonwealth penny post. A man of
character and resolution, Henniker Heaton worked ceaselessly to reduce
overseas postal rates, rallying his fellow Conservative MPs and making
powerful speeches in the House of Commons. At first he was taken only half-
seriously, as the British could not really be bothered with overseas postage.
But hard-line Henniker Heaton was undeterred and formed the League for
Universal Penny Postage in 1905.

Three years later the USA, who annually received eighteen million British

Hero's Welcome. A housemaid and members of the kitchen staff greet the postman on a cold, snow-laden morning

letters, offered the government a penny rate. But, fearing a loss of revenue, the Post Office opposed it. The government overruled them and the new rate was introduced. It was the first victory in Henniker Heaton's quest to make all letters 'as easy as speech, and as free as air'. In 1911 he achieved a penny rate for Australia and gained several more foreign concessions, but he ultimately failed to achieve an international penny rate for all member-countries of the UPU. However, his work had not gone unheeded and he was made a baronet in 1912.

A Seal of Approval

When King Edward VII came to the throne in 1901, he faced a postal dilemma. Should he follow his mother, Queen Victoria's example and pay for postage, or bring back the free royal post of her predecessors? Though he

Size Unlimited. The tallest and shortest postmen at Ramsgate post office in 1905

respected his mother's principles, King Edward was more of a traditionalist by nature who enjoyed the ritual of putting a royal wax seal on his letters. So he reintroduced the 'royal' mail.

Ever since the reign of King Edward IV, British monarchs have enjoyed free postage, the first official court post being set up in 1565 by Queen Elizabeth I for her own use. Court posts continued to seal the royal family's letters until 1840, when Queen Victoria revoked her royal rights and often posted her letters at Crathie post office near Balmoral Castle (see Chapter 8).

When King Edward re-adopted the royal seal, he opened royal post offices at Buckingham Palace and Windsor Castle, so that any member of his court could use them. Any royal servant who failed to do so was given a severe reprimand. Soon afterwards royal mail took to the air when King George V received his first coronation letters via a flight from Hendon airport to Windsor Castle (see Chapter 9). The royal service completed its geographical metamorphosis when a post office was built on the sea-going Royal Yacht *Britannia*.

The Post Office at War

There was one twentieth-century postal topic that failed to win a seal of approval, however. Letter-spying had been allegedly going on for centuries, but like many political issues no one could be quite sure about the reports' credibility. It was said to have started with the black cabinets – or *les cabinets noirs* – of the early European posts, and later adopted by Oliver Cromwell, who employed his own government letter-opener (see Chapter 2). In the seventeenth century King Louis XIV of France is reported to have used his *cabinet noir* to find out which of his courtiers were having amorous affairs; while King Charles VI of Austria put hideouts in receiving-houses to discover details of enemy plots. During their short reign from 1688–1702, Britain's King William and Queen Mary are said to have used a secret letter-opening office, which led many a merchant to complain about 'unforeseen' delays in his incoming mail. The last major incident occurred in 1844 when the home secretary Sir James Graham opened the letters of the Italian exile Mazzini (see Chapter 8).

However, in 1908 a new Letter Consolidation Act was passed allowing the government to open letters 'in very special circumstances in obedience to an express warrant in writing under the hand of a Secretary of State'. This was in effect an open invitation to the government to read private letters, a practice only really approved of during war-time.

Then in 1914 war really did break out and letter-spying – or interception – became an essential guide to enemy tactics. Letters were also used for a game of double-bluff, for knowing they would be intercepted by the German Gestapo, the British government sent counterfeit letters with morale-lowering messages about Hitler being shot or the German government falling which were then dropped behind enemy lines. To make the counterfeits more authentic, they were often put into German mail-bags that had been snatched from German trains.

At the start of the First World War the Post Office was flourishing. Its profits in 1914 were £22m and its 250,000-strong workforce was handling eleven million letters, postcards, newspapers, parcels and printed matter per day. Suddenly, however, it was facing disruption. Many of its employees were recruited for the war effort, women clerks, telegraphists and telephonists becoming nursing auxiliaries, ambulance drivers, assemblers in munitions factories and emergency telephone operators, while most of the male employees went into the forces or else worked in radar, radio and telecommunications. A mere skeleton of a postal force remained, a special unit of four thousand employees was seconded to an Army post office in the Midlands to handle and sort mail to and from the overseas forces.

During the war ten thousand members of the GPO'S own battalion, the Post Office Rifles, saw action in the bloody French battle of Flanders. It took a heavy toll; 1,836 Riflemen were killed and 3,700 wounded. Originally formed in 1796, the battalion is part of the Territorial Army. After the war a special Post Office Rifles cemetery was opened at Festubert, France, for those killed in the fighting. Of the survivors, eight received the DSO (Distinguished Service Order). A ninth, however, performed deeds of truly heroic proportions.

Sergeant Alfred Knight was stationed in Ypres, France, in 1917 when, during an attack on a German stronghold, his platoon came under heavy machine-gun fire. Ignoring the flying bullets, Sergeant Knight ran behind the enemy position, bayoneting the gunner and capturing the machine-gun single-handed. He then ran to a second machine-gun post manned by twelve Germans, bayoneting two of them, shooting the third and causing the rest to scatter. That night, Sergeant Knight's platoon moved positions and next day attacked a fortified farm. Again Sergeant Knight, wallowing in 3 ft of mud, excelled himself, shooting six Germans dead.

However, during a spell of ferocious fighting, all the British platoon's officers were killed or wounded. Assuming command, Sgt Knight rallied the depleted forces and ordered them to take up a position on the farm's left flank. After several minutes of intense shell-fire, the platoon succeeded in capturing the enemy-occupied farm. Sergeant Knight, a clerk at the GPO's North Midlands Engineering Branch, in Nottingham, was awarded the Victoria Cross and received a citation in the London Gazette for his 'exceptional bravery and initiative'.

The skeleton Post Office, meanwhile, had a quiet war. Little foreign mail was sent by air or sea and the telephone was only used in emergencies. The casualty list was high, with many post and sorting-offices and telephone exchanges destroyed and more than ten thousand employees killed or injured in the fighting.

Between the Wars

Determined to revive the battered Post Office and its falling revenues, the post-war coalition government abolished the penny post – for the first time since 1840. All letters under 4 oz now cost 1½*d*, later rising to 2*d* in 1920; telegram charges rose from 6*d* to 9*d* for twelve words; and the newspaper rate went up from ½*d* to 1*d* for items weighing up to 6 oz.

Next, with an eye more on votes than the public good, David Lloyd-George's government set up a Post Office Advisory Council to bring the GPO into closer contact with the public. Its members who included businessmen and traders carried out a pilot study on high street banking for small savers, an idea that was realized in 1968 with the founding of Girobank. The Council was really a type of consumers' organization catering for the needs of the modern man in the street who could buy and cash postal orders, collect his or her old-age pension, buy a life assurance policy, national insurance stamps and postage stamps, as well as post a letter at his or her local post office.

A House of Commons Select Committee, appointed to look at the role of telephones and telegraphs, recommended that they become a separate network. Sixty-two years later, the Committee's advice was acted upon.

There was to be yet more streamlining. In 1922 a secretariat was brought in

No. 16.

BOOKS & MAGAZINES

FOR

SOLDIERS & SAILORS.

THE public are urgently requested to hand in at any Post Office

BOOKS OR MAGAZINES

which they can spare, to be sent by organisations approved by the **WAR OFFICE** and **ADMIRALTY** to Soldiers and Sailors at home, or abroad, in camp, at the front, in hospital, or detained as Prisoners of War.

NO POSTAGE NEED BE PAID.

NO WRAPPING or ADDRESS NEEDED

THE NEED IS GREAT.

By Command of the Postmaster General.

GENERAL POST OFFICE,
16th August 1915.

Forces Network. The Post Office asked members of the public to bring in old books and magazines for members of the overseas forces

Role Model. The cartoon character Ally
Sloper provides a comical view of the
postmaster-general

at the GPO. As well as a Secretary and Second Secretary, Assistant Secretaries
were appointed to oversee the GPO's seven separate divisions, ranging from
Buildings and Supplies to Foreign Mails. It led to bitterness among the chosen
seven, some of whom believed themselves to be more equal than others. So
four of the divisions were merged into two, creating two directors above the
assistant secretaries, which managed to satisfy the ambitions of two of the
more precocious secretaries. Next the role of the Post Office's top man,
the Postmaster-General, came under scrutiny. From 1900 to 1914 the PMG
was a senior member of the cabinet. After the war the post was demoted to
junior cabinet minister level, and was usually given to young up-and-coming
politicians or older ones nearing retirement, which prompted the 1922 PMG,
Neville Chamberlain, to refer to it as one of 'comfortable obscurity'. However,
after a long debate, the government decided not to alter the PMG's role.

It was left to Viscount William Wolmer, assistant PMG from 1924 to 1929,
to make the first move. He argued that the PMG's role should be non-political,
particularly as the Post Office had become such a public institution. He also
felt strongly about the government's habit of taking money from a public
institution's coffers, which he said had turned the GPO into 'the milch-cow of

the Treasury'. In 1932 Wolmer produced a report 'Post Office Reform: Its Importance and Practicability' (the same title as Rowland Hill's), calling for the GPO to operate like a business, with dynamic leadership, high salaries and competitive entry exams.

Like Hill's before it, Wolmer's report received an enthusiastic reception from both press and public, and was supported by a petition signed by 320 MPs. The campaign led to the setting up of a public inquiry. Chaired by former Home Secretary Lord William Bridgeman, it recommended that the GPO, though still part of the civil service, should be run like a large public corporation with a board headed by the PMG and served by a chief executive instead of a secretary.

As a result, in 1934, Sir Kingsley Wood was appointed PMG, Sir Donald Banks became his new chief executive, replacing outgoing secretary Sir Evelyn Murray, and St Martin's-le-Grand was divided into three departments – postal services, telephones and telegraphs – with six smaller sub-divisions. The government also appointed ten regional directors with their own boards. The new PMG then highlighted the changes with a colourful public relations campaign, putting up large posters of cheerful-looking post offices with the

Business Brain. Viscount Wolmer produced a report 'Post Office Reform', in which he said the GPO should be run like a contemporary American company

slogan 'a brighter place for you'. The reforms seem to have had some effect. Postal volumes rose for the first time since the war and delivery rates accelerated.

At the same time, the overseas post was benefiting from advances in air travel. The transatlantic service boomed, the passage to India could be made with only one stopover, and the flying boat made the carrying of bulk cargo items easier. To mark the air revolution, the GPO put up a number of blue post-boxes for airmail letters, but, fearing they were secret service devices, the British public failed to use them. So they were taken down again.

The Post Office at War Again

When war was declared in September 1939 an optimistic PMG, Mr Herbert Morrison, told the public: 'Hitler shall not spoil a British Christmas Post'. And he didn't. That year's Christmas post was just like any other, with large squads of part-timers tramping the cities, towns and villages with the Christmas parcels, letters and cards amid the traditional bustle and merriment of the festive season.

As before, most of the Post Office's male employees joined the forces. The inland post continued in a small way, with many of its tasks being carried out by women. However, there was little overseas traffic, items often taking several months to reach their destinations. Yet the war brought an unexpected bonus to the letter-writing public. The airgraph – a 100 ft length of photographic film carrying seventeen hundred messages – was a boon for overseas post. Light, neat and easy to stow in an aeroplane hold, it could be developed like a normal camera film and read by its many recipients. It often enabled regiments of a thousand or more servicemen to receive news of their families and to send replies in kind.

Another war-time winner was the airmail letter. This new space-saver was a one-off, combining writing space, with envelope and stamp on a single sheet of paper. The first, posted in Cairo on 21 April 1941, reached London on 13 May. At first the air letter was restricted to members of the armed forces, but recognizing its popularity, the government opened the service to the public, and in 1943 61 million were sent, soaring to 135 million the next year, and, perhaps inevitably, catching on worldwide.

Again, letter interception played a vital war-time role. A series of German

Next Please. A local resident posts a letter in a Victorian post-box at Buxton, Derbyshire, in 1935

Woman's Role. One of the many women
recruited for postal work during the Second
World War

letters confiscated by the government enabled Sir Winston Churchill's War
Cabinet to discover the Germans' detailed plans for the D-Day Landings. Thus
the government was able to make early preparations for the attempted
invasion. The Germans employed similar tactics, and, as a precaution, all
letters sent to the British forces in Germany were censored by a senior Army
officer in case they betrayed tactical secrets.

The war was to take a heavy toll. The biggest loss was the bombing of the
Central Telegraph Office at St Paul's, London, in 1940. But, their backs
against the wall, engineers and builders rebuilt it in three weeks! As before,
many post-boxes, offices and exchanges were destroyed, and casualties
reached the ten thousand mark. In city areas of particularly heavy bombing,
mobile units were used to sort, collect and deliver the mail.

The Christmas post, however continued to boom, the GPO each year taking
on up to seventy thousand part-timers, including a large number of married
couples, to help sort and deliver. The sight of Mr and Mrs Postman trudging up
the snow-laden front path with their bundles of Christmas post became a
familiar feature for local home-owners.

Mobile Patrol. One of the emergency post offices used in areas of heavy bombing during the Second World War

The second Christmas of the war marked a remarkable anniversary – it was the forty-fifth year that 68-year-old postwoman Miss Jane Preston had worked her postal round in Cockerham, Lancashire, during which she covered a total of 140,000 miles wearing wooden clogs! During her retirement speech a few years later, Miss Preston said she was delighted to put her feet up at last.

16
Microchips with Everything

And now I see with eye serene, The very pulse of the machine; A being breathing thoughtful breath, A traveller between life and death.

William Wordsworth (1770–1850)

Britain and its resources were severely drained by the Second World War. The country faced a long, hazardous climb back to stability and hard-hit institutions like the Post Office had to cope with costly rebuilding programmes. There was no quick cure. The GPO's workforce had been drastically reduced, postal revenues had plunged and the public had lost the spark to write letters.

So yet again, war had changed the post. During the Greek and Roman Empires, great battles helped to forge new postal routes and teams of couriers, and even the English civil wars moulded a vigorous band of royal postmen. Then war became more perverse. In both the American Civil War and the Napoleonic Wars, valuable packet-ships were lost in skirmishes with privateers, and the Post Office was used as a convenient funding-agency by the British government. Later the two great wars took an even greater toll on the Post Office, though once again Britains's victories were boosted by GPO funds.

In its post-war recovery programme in 1940, the GPO made recruitment its first priority. However, it found it had been upstaged by the 1944 Education Act. The school leaving age had been raised from fourteen to sixteen years, reducing the number of youngsters available for telegram delivery, messenger and auxiliary work; while the sixteen-year-old school leavers who had previously worked as postmen or women and sorters now stayed on at school to qualify for a university or college education; finally, the GPO's third labour source – low income earners who worked part-time to gain a few extra pounds – could now claim social security benefit instead. There was almost full employment, and with the safety of social security behind them, job-seekers no longer felt the need to opt for a solid, secure job-for-life at the Post Office. The GPO faced a dilemma.

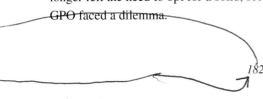

182

However, despite the gloomy outlook, the Post Office made a profit for the next ten years. Then came the crunch. In 1955 profits turned to losses. GPO administrators scratched around for solutions, organizing departmental fact-finding studies and recruiting a succession of economics professors to pass on useful tips. Suddenly they made a startling discovery: 66 per cent of the Post Office's expenditure went on wages and salaries. The GPO was too labour-intensive. The solution was mechanization.

The Segregator

The contemporary letter was sorted three times. First it was taken to the local district sorting-office and sorted according to its destination; then it was sent to its second sorting-office and allotted a town or village; finally it went to another department where it was given its precise street of delivery. This was a relatively slow process and, during the 1950s, scientists at the GPO laboratories in Dollis Hill, London, experimented with mechanical methods of sorting. Finally they came up with the segregator. It was put to the test at Redhill sorting-office, Surrey, where it more than proved its worth and was rapidly introduced throughout the rest of country.

The new machine was in fact a revolving drum. All outward-going letters, packets and parcels were carried by conveyor-belt to the drum which whirled them round, dropping the letters through a series of slots in the side and carrying the parcels and packets to another part of the sorting-office.

Soon, segregators were used only for letters, while parcels and packets were carried on moving sorting-machines that could pre-sort fifteen hundred items an hour. Then the segregator was replaced by the high-speed E.40 letter sorting-machine.

The Postcode

Now scientists needed to streamline the next stage of mail-sorting. They invented a little device called the postcode – a sequence of six digits that could pinpoint the exact destination of any item. Pre-sorted letters and parcels were sent to a coding operator who typed each item's postcode in phosphorescent dots above and below the address, the top half showing the town or district of destination, and the bottom, the precise street. It proved a highly effective

Machines speeded up the sorting process in the 1950s. Here are four current devices: Opposite above: The OCR – or electronic eye – that reads printed or typed postcodes to help speed letters on their way; Opposite below: The E.40 sorting machine that reads the coded destination of letters; Above: The NP4000 sorting machine that can handle up to thirty-two thousand letters an hour; Below: The coding desk at London's Mount Pleasant sorting-office where operators read handwritten postcodes

labour-saver until a little electronic eye came on the scene. Known as the OCR (optical character recognition) machine, it could read typed and printed addresses and postcodes, printing out coded destinations on the envelopes at the rate of thirty-five thousand an hour. Handwritten codes continued to be read by operators.

Then the GPO put their public relations talents to the test. Needing to make the postcode public, they introduced it at the East Anglian town of Norwich in 1959. During the first week more than half the town forgot to use the code, and the Post Office began to have second thoughts. But they persisted and finally, after two months, almost all Norwich's correspondents were using postcodes. The scheme went national, each mail item being franked with the words: 'Please Use The Postcode'.

The Post Office are now introducing OCR videos that can read both handwritten and printed codes, and an NP4000 sorting machine which can read the phosphorescent dots on thirty-two thousand items an hour and bag them ready for their final destination.

Other Innovations

Mechanization had successfully replaced men and women with machines. The Post Office now set about recruiting teams of specialists to run the new technology and organized training schemes for existing employees. But harsh facts had to be faced – every year since 1955 the GPO had been making a loss. There were gaps that needed plugging.

One of them was finance, and in 1960 a government White Paper 'The Status of the Post Office' made a promising start. Instead of having to consult the Treasury over financial decisions, the GPO was given its own central fund, or kitty, managed by the postmaster-general, into which it could pay its takings and draw any expenditure it needed. The move saved many hours of paperwork.

Britain's rural regions were also losing money for the GPO. To improve services and boost revenues, the GPO introduced delivery vans and motor cycles in areas where postmen had been facing long, tiring treks, while in more remote regions, a parcel van that doubled as a bus was put into service. The first post-buses, which could make parcel deliveries and carry sixteen passengers at the same time, ran between Lanidloes and Llangurig in South Wales, followed by services in the north of Scotland, the Scottish Isles, mid-

Wales and the south-west of England. The buses, which resembled large, red post-office vans, were invaluable in isolated areas, carrying pensioners, the disabled and unemployed, householders wishing to visit their nearest shop or shops, children travelling to and from school, and even running conducted tours for tourists and visitors. They could also carry passengers on local bus routes that had been closed due to lack of demand.

Two-tier Postage

In 1968 the government prescribed a new remedy for the loss-making GPO – two-tier postage. At the time, the plan seemed almost too far-fetched for GPO management, for it meant grading all postage as first- or second-class mail and seemed a nightmarish prospect for the already overworked sorting-offices. But the GPO were willing to try anything to get out of debt.

The idea was that all urgent items would travel first class, getting priority treatment in the sorting-offices, so that they could be delivered the day after posting. Meanwhile less urgent mail was marked 'second class' and delivered after two or three days. All letters would now carry first- or second-class stamps. However, instead of over-burdening the sorting-offices, it was found that a slow- and fast-lane system simplified sorting, relieved peak-hour congestion and saved manpower. After several weeks of experiment, the plan went ahead.

Now, when letters arrived for their first sorting, they were fed into an Automatic Letter Facer, known as ALF, read by an electronic scanner and divided into their first- and second-class categories. The letters were then cancelled (i.e. marked with the date and town) ready to be coded.

To ease the sorting process further, many post-boxes were equipped with first- and second-class slots, a system that was later adopted by the European posts, though one Italian town introduced post-boxes with the first- and second-class slots leading into the same compartment!

The government's second radical measure of 1968 was the founding of Girobank, or the 'people's money-box', after a survey found that only 50 per cent of the public had a bank account. The Girobank system, which kept its records on a giant computer in Bootle, near Liverpol, was introduced in all high street post offices, and gave almost two million customers their first taste of cheque-signing.

Mystery Mail

With their new reforms in place, the government and the Post Office looked for further economies. Since 1784 the GPO had kept a large department known as the Dead Letter Office at Mount Pleasant, London's largest and busiest sorting-office. But the sorting-office needed the space, so the DLO moved to new offices in Portsmouth in 1969.

The DLO – sometimes known as the returned letter office – handles all mail that cannot be found a home, i.e. wrongly-addressed items, ones that have got lost in the system, or those whose recipients have moved or died. Handling 'dead' letters is no easy task, and the DLO has its own Brains Trust to uncover clues to letters' hidden pasts.

Sometimes the Brains Trust get lucky, simply opening the mystery letter, and finding the name of the sender or recipient inside. On other occasions, the task can resemble the twists and ironies of a Sherlock Holmes novel. In such cases, greater resources are needed, and the Brains Trust have a research

Mystery Men. Members of the Dead Letter Office examine the contents of an unidentified parcel

department, where they can use microscopes and laboratory-testing equipment and, if that fails, sift through encyclopaedias, maps and reference books in their search for clues. Occasionally, when letters arrive with addresses written in invisible ink, the Brains Trust have to resort to the good old-fashioned kettle, dangling them over the steam to reveal their true identities.

Recent DLO items have included a cardboard-box filled with live snakes, a baby monkey, two human skulls, a box containing thirty-three tree-frogs, still alive and hopping, and an unaddressed parcel from Paris with a purring Burmese kitten inside. Whatever the item, the DLO has a fairly high success rate, and members are always sad when they have to finally pronounce an item 'dead'.

Postmen's Riddles

Clever postmen sometimes do their own detection work. In 1965 a letter marked 'WD and HO' was correctly delivered to the head office of the tobacco makers W.D. and H.O. Wills in Bristol, while a Russian letter addressed 'Nine Feet Eight, The Circus, London' was subsequently handed to a giant appearing in a Russian touring troupe at London's Hippodrome Theatre. Some addresses appear in the form of riddles, like this one that arrived at a Middlesex sorting-office:

> To Rita, whose surname and house
> All resemble rising ground
> Pleasant is the Mount she calls her home
> Near a famed boy's school is to be found.

Several puzzled postmen eventually traced the address to Miss Rita Berkeley-Hill, 4 Mount Pleasant, Harrow-on-the-Hill, Middlesex, which is near Harrow public school. Two others were addressed:

> Dennis Belcher, Mill Street, Co Cork,
> As you turn the corner to Tom Mantel's field
> Where Jack Gallaghan's horse was drowned in the bog-hole.

> To my sister Jean,
> Up the Canongate,

Down a close,

Edinburgh.

She has a wooden leg.

Senders can be very demanding. In 1986 a Tunbridge Wells postmaster received a letter from an American businessman asking him where he could buy ten camels as he had heard rumours that the Kent roads were unsuitable for cars, and in 1970 an Eastbourne postmaster was asked by a Swedish naturalist to send samples of rare plants growing in the area.

Once in a while a letter gets lodged in the system. A job application written by a trainee solicitor in 1949, turned up at a well-known firm of London solicitors in 1989, forty years late, by which time the sender had not only qualified as a solicitor and enjoyed a successful career, but retired.

The Post Office goes Public

In 1969 the Post Office went public. The Act making it a public corporation was passed by Harold Wilson's Labour government after three years of legislation. Labour believed a public Post Office would serve the needs of the consumer and operate more efficiently on the open market than a civil service department.

The GPO became two large organizations – telephones and posts. Specialist interests such as national savings stamps and broadcasting licences were taken over by the government. Meanwhile, the PMG and his officials were replaced by a new team of decision-makers, a chairman, Lord Leonard Hall and a six-man board. The outgoing PMG, John Stonehouse, said:

> In the communications explosion we shall be experiencing during the next ten years, there will be a public authority fully able to take advantage of the commercial opportunities available to it, to service the public and provide new ways of improving communications within the United Kingdom.

The Masters of Despatch

However, not everyone was satisfied with the new 'communications explosion'. The GPO's three key unions went on strike for three weeks when their 15 per cent pay claim was turned down by management in 1971. But the 1970s were that sort of decade. Industrial output was low, inflation high, there were many wage freezes, and the Post Office was still losing money. The remedies were running out, though a flicker of hope shone when the GPO opened a marketing department with strict instructions to produce as many money-making ideas as possible. It was only a flicker, for in 1974 the Post Office lost £100m. And when it raised its stamp prices, the measure had little effect. For in 1977 two billion less items were sent than in 1967.

It was left to the Post Office Review Committee, chaired by Charles Carter, Vice-Chancellor of Lancaster University, to raise the tempo, when it devised two big money-spinners – direct mail and discounts for large companies. The formula worked and by 1978 the Post Office was making a profit for the first time since 1955. Suddenly Britain's economy started prospering, and as we have seen throughout history, the Post Office followed suit, its volumes rising at the rate of 12 per cent per year.

Meanwhile, the Post Office's telephones department – now known as telecommunications – had swelled into a huge network, and in 1981 Margaret Thatcher's Conservative government passed the British Telecommunications Act, creating a new public corporation, British Telecom, based at Gresham Street, London, with its own chairman, board and regional offices. The following year, a separate company, Post Office Counters, was formed to run post offices, offering a new range of services including bus-passes, electricity and gas savings stamps, and stationery. It is now the largest chain of retail outlets in Europe.

The Post Office had come out of its post-war hibernation. Its two hundred thousand workforce took home a far smaller proportion of its profits, volumes were continuing to rise, and GPO headquarters had swelled beyond its boundaries. In 1985 it moved from St Martin's-le-Grand to a large Victorian mansion in Grosvenor Place, London.

In 1986 a 'Corporate Plan' recommended that the Post Office be streamlined into four separate commercial-style companies consisting of Royal Mail Letters, Royal Mail Parcels (Parcelforce), the existing Post Office Counters, which later became a limited company, and Girobank Ltd, each headed by a managing director and served by separate finance, marketing and engineering divisions. The plan went ahead and two further boards were set up to run the Scottish and Welsh posts in Edinburgh and Cardiff, respectively. The same

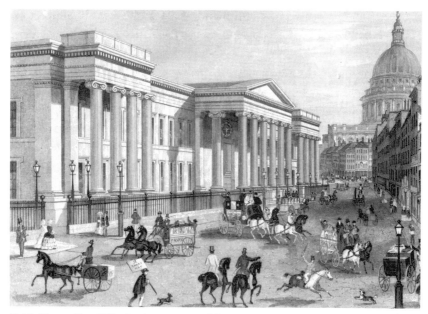

Quick Change. Post Office headquarters moved from St Martin's-le-Grand (above) to Grosvenor Place (below) in central London in 1985. Seven years later it transferred to Old Street in the City

year a £4m GPO research centre was opened at Swindon. Equipped with laboratories, computer rooms and testing equipment, it started producing new technology for both home use and export.

By 1988 the GPO's annual pre-tax profit was £167m. It was now delivering fifty-five million items a day and coping with an intense workload. However, it prudently continued to economize, closing a number of loss-making high street post offices and opening postal franchises in supermarkets and large stores. At the same time a campaign led by the Post Office and the Post Office Users National Council created a new local service, the community post office. Individuals living in remote villages and shires volunteered to use their homes, pubs or local clubs as post offices for twenty hours a week in return for an annual retainer. Many of them resembled the friendly Victorian post office where customers enjoyed exchanging a bit of gossip with their daily business. A typical example is Britain's highest post office in the village of Flash, perched delicately on a 1,500 ft tor in the Derbyshire Peak District. Each day postmistress Mrs Kathy Phillips hands out cups of tea over postal transactions in her kitchen, to the melodic accompaniment of mooing cows and cackling goats in an adjoining garage. She even provides transport – hiring out a bicycle to anyone facing a long trek home.

In 1990 Post Office Parcels changed its name to Parcelforce. Despite fierce competition from its many rivals, it became Britain's number one carrier and by mid-1991 had turned a recession-led loss into profit. In 1991 the Post Office launched a £2.2 billion project to replace part-mechanized sorting-offices with seventy-five fully automated processing centres by 1996. Meanwhile in high street post offices, electronic tills helped relieve an increasing workload and, for connoisseurs, post-shops and collection centres started offering own brand stationery, stamps and coins.

In 1992 personal computers and electronic scales were introduced to speed up daily transactions in post offices. The year also marked a classic case of the seven year itch. After moving from St Martin's-le-Grand to Grosvenor Place in 1985, Post Office headquarters and Royal Mail Letters transferred again this time to Old Street in the city of London, while Post Office Counters went to nearby Greville Street and Parcelforce established a new base at Milton Keynes.

The Post Office's economy drive had succeeded. In 1993, after seventeen successive years of profit-making, it achieved its highest-ever annual total of

£283m, handling a record twenty-two billion items – one per day for each member of the public. But once again history repeated itself when the government announced it was taking a larger share of postal profits for public spending. The 1993 contribution was £68m, with £181m targeted for 1994, £176m in 1995 and a total of £158m in 1996. The GPO chairman, Michael Heron, said the Post Office had once again been 'caught in the bizarre world of the cash-based Public Sector Borrowing Requirement'. Once again it faced short-term planning and low capital investment, and once again it had become the 'milch-cow of the Treasury'.

It is an anomaly that can only be solved by Post Office reform or privatization. Meanwhile, a hundred and twenty thousand postmen and women thread round Britain's streets and by-ways, a hundred thousand post-boxes stand like red sentinels on busy street corners and sleepy country lanes, and more than twenty thousand post and sub-post offices cater for the needs of a growing, product-conscious population.

The British Post Office is a world leader once more. And what could be more typically British than to meet the neighbours in the local sub-post office, discuss the latest petrol prices, Mrs Crawford's crazy hairstyle, the mysterious hole in the pavement outside Mr Lamb the Butcher's, and, of course, post that long-promised letter to Uncle Derek?

References

Place of publication given only if outside London.

Clinton, Alan, *Post Office Workers: A Trade Union and Social History*. George Allen and Unwin, 1984.

Daunton, Martin J., *Royal Mail: The Post Office Since 1840*. Athlone, 1985.

Farrugia, Jean Young, *The Letter Box*. Fontwell (Centaur Press Ltd), 1969.

——, *The Life and Work of Sir Rowland Hill, 1795–1879*. National Postal Museum, 1979.

Farrugia, Jean Young and Gammons, Tony, *Carrying British Mails*. National Postal Museum, 1980.

Gammons, Tony, *The Early Days of the Postal Service*. British Philatelic Bureau, 1986.

Griffiths, T.A.Q., 'Development of Rural Postal Services with particular reference to Devon 1790–1905.' Exeter University thesis, 1986.

Hyde, James Wilson, *The Royal Mail*. Simpkin, Marshall, 1889.

Lewins, William, *Her Majesty's Mails*. Sampson, Low and Marston, 1864.

Martin, Nancy, *The Post Office*. J.M. Dent, 1969.

Post Office Archives. Original documents. Freeling House, Mount Pleasant, London, EC1A 1BB.

Robinson, Howard, *The British Post Office*. Princeton University Press, 1948.

——, *Carrying British Mails Overseas*. Allen and Unwin, 1964.

Trollope, Anthony, *An Autobiography*. Oxford, OUP, 1950 (originally published 1883).

Worlock, David, *Post Haste!* Thomas Nelson, 1972.

Zilliacus, Laurin, *From Pillar to Post: The Troubled History of the Mail*. Heinemann, 1956.

Index